KU-637-676

cooking chinese

cooking chinese

KATHY MAN

HERMES HOUSE

For all recipes, **quantities** are given in both **metric** & **imperial** measures &, where appropriate, measures are also given in **standard cups** & **spoons**. Follow one set, but not a mixture, because they are **not interchangeable**.

Standard **spoon** & **cup measures** are level.
1 tsp = 5 ml, 1 tbsp = 15 ml, 1 cup = 250 ml/8 fl oz

Australian standard **tablespoons** are 20 ml. Australian readers should use 3 tsp in place of 1 tbsp for measuring small quantities of gelatine, cornflour, salt, etc.

Medium eggs are used unless otherwise stated.

Some of the recipes in this book previously appeared in **Step-by-Step Low Fat Chinese**.

First published in 1999 by Hermes House

© Anness Publishing Limited 1999

Hermes House is an imprint of Anness Publishing Limited
Hermes House, 88–89 Blackfriars Road, London SE1 8HA

All rights reserved. No part of this publication may be reproduced, stored in a retrieval system or transmitted in any way or by any means, electronic, mechanical, photocopying, recording or otherwise, without the prior written permission of the copyright holder.

ISBN 1-84038-498-0

A CIP catalogue record for this book is available from the British Library

Publisher Joanna Lorenz
Senior editor Doreen Palamartschuk
Copy editors Linda Doeser & Jenni Fleetwood
Photography William Lingwood, Dave King, Nicki Dowey
Design Wherefore Art?
Styling Clare Louise Hunt & Clare Reynolds
Food for photography Lucy McKelvie, Jennie Shapter, Becky Johnson
Production controller Karina Han

Printed & bound in Singapore
10 9 8 7 6 5 4 3 2 1

687701
MORAY COUNCIL
DEPARTMENT OF TECHNICAL
& LEISURE SERVICES
641.595

introduction

Delicious dishes from this **popular** cuisine, that can be cooked in minutes – what could be better for the **modern cook?** The recipes are a unique and **tempting** collection and a combination of **irresistible** favourites with refreshingly new tastes and **textures. Quick** and **easy** to prepare, these simple dishes capture the **authentic flavours** of this superb cuisine to give **spectular results** for entertaining and every occasion.

flavourings & spices

CHINESE COOKING IS SO **POPULAR** THAT EVEN SMALL SUPERMARKETS TEND TO **STOCK** AN **EXTENSIVE SELECTION** OF **FLAVOURING** INGREDIENTS.

BLACK BEAN SAUCE

This sauce is made from salted fermented soy beans, which have been crushed and mixed to a thick paste with flavourings. Black bean sauce is highly concentrated and is usually added to hot oil at the start of cooking to release the flavour.

YELLOW BEAN SAUCE

A puree of fermented yellow beans combined with salt, flour and sugar. This is a thick, sweetish, smooth sauce and is often used in marinades.

CHILLIES

A wide variety of these hot members of the capsicum family is available. They are most used for flavouring, but plump ones can be stuffed and served as a vegetable once the fiery seeds have been removed.

CHILLI OIL

This reddish vegetable oil owes both its colour and spicy flavour to the chillies that have been steeped or marinated in it. Use chilli oil sparingly in cooking or as a peppery dipping sauce.

DRIED SHRIMPS

Dried, salty shrimps used as a flavouring and also as an ingredient. The shrimps are always soaked in warm water first to remove some of the salt. They have a strong flavour, so should be used sparingly.

FIVE-SPICE POWDER

A finely ground mixture of fennel seeds, star anise, Sichuan peppercorns, cloves and cinnamon. It has a fairly strong liquor taste and a pungent spicy aroma and should be used sparingly. It can be used in both sweet and savoury dishes.

GARLIC

This small, aromatic vegetable is one of the most important flavouring ingredients in Chinese cooking. The most common method of preparing garlic is to peel it, then chop it finely or mince it. However, garlic is sometimes simply bruised, or peeled and sliced.

GINGER

Fresh root ginger is an essential flavouring ingredient in Chinese cooking. It is peeled, then sliced, shredded or minced before use. Dried ginger or ground ginger does not have the same fresh flavour and is not suitable as a substitute. Fresh root ginger freezes well. Keep a well-wrapped, peeled root in the freezer and grate it as required. It will thaw instantly.

HOISIN SAUCE

A thick, rich, dark sauce often used for flavouring meat and poultry before cooking. It is also sometimes used as one of the ingredients in a dipping sauce.

LOTUS LEAVES

The dried leaves of the lotus plant are used as an aromatic wrapping for steamed dishes. Lotus leaves must be soaked in water for 30 minutes to soften them before use.

OYSTER SAUCE

This thick, dark sauce is made from oyster juice, flour, salt and sugar. It is usually added to dishes at the end of cooking.

RICE VINEGAR

A colourless, slightly sweet vinegar used to add sharpness to sweet-and-sour dishes. If rice vinegar is not obtainable, white vinegar or cider vinegar sweetened with sugar can be used as a substitute.

ROCK SUGAR

An aptly-named ingredient that consists of irregular lumps of amber-coloured sugar. Derived from sugar cane, rock sugar is mainly used in sweet dishes and has a caramelized flavour.

SESAME OIL

This aromatic oil is made from roasted sesame seeds. Small quantities are used as an accent at the end of cooking to add flavour to a dish; in Chinese cooking it is not used for frying.

DARK SOY SAUCE

A rich, dark sauce that is used to add both colour and flavour to many sauces and marinades. Dark soy sauce is quite salty and is often used instead of salt to season a dish.

LIGHT SOY SAUCE

A thin, dark sauce used for flavouring many Chinese dishes and also as a table condiment. The flavour is slightly lighter and fresher than dark soy sauce, but it is a little more salty.

STAR ANISE

A strong liquorice-tasting spice mainly used to flavour meat and poultry. The whole spice is frequently used in braised dishes so that the flavour can be released and absorbed slowly.

vegetables & mushrooms

beans & bean products

AUTHENTIC INGREDIENTS MAKE ALL THE **DIFFERENCE**. LOOK OUT FOR **THESE** AT **ORIENTAL** MARKETS.

PACKED WITH **PROTEIN**, THESE ARE ESSENTIAL INGREDIENTS THAT **NO SELF-RESPECTING** CHINESE **COOK** SHOULD **BE WITHOUT**.

BAMBOO SHOOTS

Crunchy young shoots from the bamboo plant, these have a delicate, but distinctive flavour. They are available in cans, either whole, sliced or cut into thin, matchstick-size shreds.

CHINESE MUSHROOMS

When fresh, they are sold as shiitake mushrooms, but the dried version is more widely used in Chinese cooking. Dried Chinese mushrooms have a more concentrated flavour. Soak in hot water before use.

CLOUD EARS, WOOD EARS

Dried edible fungi that have a crunchy texture; cloud ears have a more delicate flavour than wood ears. Once reconstituted in water they expand to many times their original size.

STRAW MUSHROOMS

These are grown on rice straw and have a slippery, meaty texture with little flavour. At present these mushrooms are only available canned. In Chinese cooking, they are used mainly for their texture.

LOTUS ROOT

A crunchy vegetable with naturally occurring holes, lotus root is occasionally sold fresh, but is more frequently available dried or frozen. When cut and pulled apart, thread-like strands are produced from the cut surfaces. Also known as renkon.

TARO

A starchy tuber used in both savoury and sweet dishes. It looks like a hairy swede with white flesh slightly marked by purplish dots. The flavour and texture resemble those of a floury potato.

WATER CHESTNUTS

Once peeled, these black-skinned bulbs reveal a white, crunchy interior with a sweet flavour. Canned, peeled water chestnuts are available in most supermarkets, but the fresh, unpeeled bulb can sometimes be bought in Chinese stores.

ADUKI BEANS

Small red beans used mainly in sweet dishes. As with most pulses, aduki beans must be soaked in water before use. They should be boiled hard for 10 minutes at the start of cooking, then simmered until soft before use.

TOFU (BEANCURD)

As its name suggests, this is a cheese-like product made from soya beans. Fresh tofu (beancurd) is sold covered in water. It has very little flavour of its own, but readily absorbs flavourings. Tofu (beancurd) is used extensively in Chinese cooking and is a good source of protein. There are several different types, including "silken" tofu and smoked tofu, but the firm variety is the one normally used by the Chinese.

DRIED TOFU (BEANCURD) STICKS

These are sheets of tofu (beancurd), which have been formed into sticks and dried. They are an important ingredient in Chinese vegetarian dishes. They must be soaked in hot water before being used. Tofu (beancurd) sticks are usually available only in Chinese supermarkets.

A

B

C

A: From top left, bamboo shoots, the large tuber known as taro, lotus root with its naturally occurring holes and water chestnuts.

B: From top left, fresh shiitake mushrooms, canned straw mushrooms, dried cloud ears and Chinese mushrooms.

C: Aduki beans and fresh tofu (beancurd) and dried tofu (beancurd) sticks, protein rich components of many Chinese recipes.

soups & starters

tomato & beef soup

FRESH TOMATOES AND **SPRING ONIONS** GIVE THIS LIGHT BEEF BROTH A **SUPERB** FLAVOUR.

method

SERVES 4

1 Cut the beef into thin strips and place it in a saucepan. Pour over boiling water to cover. Cook for 2 minutes, then drain thoroughly and set aside.

2 Bring the stock to the boil in a clean pan. Stir in the tomato purée, then the tomatoes and sugar. Add the beef strips, allow the stock to boil again, then lower the heat and simmer for 2 minutes.

3 Mix the cornflour to a paste with the water. Add the mixture to the soup, stirring constantly until it thickens slightly. Lightly beat the egg white in a cup.

4 Pour the egg white into the soup in a steady stream, stirring all the time. As soon as the egg white changes colour, add salt and pepper, stir the soup and pour it into heated bowls. Drizzle each portion with a few drops of sesame oil, sprinkle with the spring onions and serve.

---

cook's tip
For the best flavour, use sun-ripened tomatoes for this soup, rather than tomatoes ripened under glass, which tend to taste insipid.

---

ingredients

75g/3oz **rump steak,** trimmed
  of fat
900ml/1½ pints/3¾ cups
  beef stock
30ml/2 tbsp **tomato purée**
6 **tomatoes,** halved, seeded
  and chopped
10ml/2 tsp **caster sugar**
15ml/1 tbsp **cornflour**
15ml/1 tbsp **cold water**
1 **egg white**
2.5ml/½ tsp **sesame oil**
2 **spring onions,** finely shredded
salt and freshly ground
  black pepper

ingredients

50g/2oz raw **tiger prawns**

50g/2oz queen **scallops**

75g/3oz skinless **cod fillet**, roughly chopped

15ml/1 tbsp finely chopped **chives**

5ml/1 tsp **dry sherry**

1 small **egg white**, lightly beaten

2.5ml/¹⁄₂tsp **sesame oil**

1.5ml/¹⁄₄tsp **salt**

large pinch of freshly ground **white pepper**

900 ml/1¹⁄₂ pints/3³⁄₄ cups **fish stock**

20 **wonton wrappers**

2 Cos **lettuce leaves,** shredded

fresh **coriander** leaves and **garlic chives**, to garnish

cook's tip

The filled wanton wrappers can be made ahead, then frozen for several weeks and cooked straight from the freezer.

seafood wonton soup

THIS IS A **VARIATION** ON THE POPULAR WONTON SOUP THAT IS **TRADITIONALLY** PREPARED USING **PORK**.

method

SERVES 4

1 Peel and devein the prawns. Rinse them well, pat them dry on kitchen paper and cut them into small pieces.

2 Rinse the scallops. Pat them dry, using kitchen paper. Chop them into small pieces the same size as the prawns.

3 Place the cod in a food processor and process until a paste is formed. Scrape into a bowl and stir in the prawns, scallops, chives, sherry, egg white, sesame oil, salt and pepper. Mix thoroughly, cover and leave in a cool place to marinate for 20 minutes.

4 Heat the fish stock gently in a saucepan. To prepare the wontons, place a teaspoonful of the seafood filling in the centre of a wonton wrapper, then bring the corners together to meet at the top. Twist them together to enclose the filling. Fill the remaining wonton wrappers in the same way.

5 Bring a large saucepan of water to the boil. Drop in the wontons. When the water returns to the boil, lower the heat and simmer gently for 5 minutes, or until the wontons float to the surface. Drain the wontons and divide them among four heated soup bowls.

6 Add a portion of lettuce to each bowl. Bring the fish stock to the boil. Ladle it into each bowl, garnish each portion with coriander leaves and garlic chives and serve immediately.

THIS **SPICY** WARMING SOUP REALLY **WHETS** THE **APPETITE** AND IS THE PERFECT **INTRODUCTION** TO A CHINESE MEAL.

ingredients

10g/¹/₄oz dried **cloud ears**

8 fresh **shiitake mushrooms**

75g/3oz **tofu** (beancurd)

50g/2oz/¹/₂ cup sliced, drained, canned **bamboo shoots**

900ml/1¹/₂ pints/3³/₄ cups **vegetable stock**

15ml/1 tbsp **caster sugar**

45ml/3 tbsp **rice vinegar**

15ml/1 tbsp **light soy sauce**

1.5ml/¹/₄ tsp **chilli oil**

2.5ml/¹/₂ tsp **salt**

large pinch of freshly ground **white pepper**

15ml/1 tbsp **cornflour**

15ml/1 tbsp **cold water**

1 **egg white**

5ml/1 tsp **sesame oil**

2 **spring onions**, cut into fine rings

hot-&-sour soup

method

SERVES 4

1 Soak the cloud ears in a bowl of hot water for 30 minutes, or until soft. Drain, trim off and discard the hard base from each and chop the cloud ears roughly.

2 Remove and discard the stalks from the shiitake mushrooms. Cut the caps into thin strips. Cut the tofu (beancurd) into 1cm/¹/₂in cubes and shred the bamboo shoots finely.

3 Place the stock, mushrooms, tofu (beancurd), bamboo shoots and cloud ears in a large saucepan. Bring the stock to the boil, lower the heat and simmer for about 5 minutes.

4 Stir in the sugar, vinegar, soy sauce, chilli oil, salt and pepper. Mix the cornflour to a paste with the water. Add the mixture to the soup, stirring constantly until it starts to thicken.

5 Lightly beat the egg white, then pour it slowly into the soup in a steady stream, stirring constantly. Cook, stirring, until the egg white changes colour.

6 Add the sesame oil just before serving. Ladle into heated bowls and top each portion with spring onion rings.

cook's tip
To transform this tasty soup into a nutritious, light meal, simply add extra mushrooms, tofu (beancurd) and bamboo shoots.

crispy turkey balls

TURKEY IS NOT TRADITIONALLY USED IN CHINESE COOKING, BUT IT MAKES A VERY **TASTY ALTERNATIVE** TO CHICKEN.

method

SERVES 4–6

1 Preheat the oven to 120°C/250°F/Gas 1/2. Brush the bread lightly with olive oil and cut it into 5mm/1/4in cubes. Spread over a baking sheet and bake for 15 minutes, until dry and crisp.

2 Meanwhile, mix together the turkey meat, water chestnuts and chillies in a food processor. Process until a coarse paste is formed.

3 Add the egg white, coriander leaves, cornflour, salt and pepper. Pour in half the soy sauce and process for about 30 seconds. Scrape into a bowl, cover and leave in a cool place for 20 minutes.

4 Remove the toasted bread from the oven and set aside. Raise the oven temperature to 200°C/400°F/Gas 6. With dampened hands, divide the turkey mixture into 12 portions and form into balls.

5 Roughly crush the toasted bread, then transfer to a plate. Roll each ball in turn over the toasted crumbs until coated. Place on a baking sheet and bake for about 20 minutes, or until the coating is brown and the turkey filling has cooked through.

6 In a small bowl, mix the remaining soy sauce with the caster sugar, rice vinegar and chilli oil. Serve the sauce with the turkey balls, garnished with shredded chillies and coriander sprigs.

ingredients

4 thin slices of **white bread**, crusts removed
5ml/1 tsp **olive oil**
225g/8oz skinless, boneless **turkey meat**, roughly chopped
50g/2oz/1/3 cup drained, canned **water chestnuts**
2 fresh **red chillies**, seeded and roughly chopped
1 **egg white**
10g/1/4oz/1/4 cup fresh **coriander** leaves
5ml/1 tsp **cornflour**
2.5ml/1/2 tsp **salt**
1.5ml/1/4 tsp freshly ground **white pepper**
30ml/2 tbsp **light soy sauce**
5ml/1 tsp **caster sugar**
30ml/2 tbsp **rice vinegar**
2.5ml/1/2 tsp **chilli oil**
shredded **red chillies** and fresh **coriander sprigs**, to garnish

> ### variation
> Chicken or pork can be used instead of turkey, with equally delicious results.

THIS **HEALTHY**
VERSION OF THE
EVER-POPULAR
STARTER HAS LOST
NONE OF ITS **CLASSIC**
CRUNCH AND TASTE.

ingredients

6 slices medium-cut **white**
   bread, crusts removed

225g/8oz raw **tiger prawns**,
   peeled and deveined

50g/2oz/1/3 cup drained, canned
   water chestnuts

1 **egg white**

5ml/1 tsp **sesame oil**

2.5ml/1/2 tsp **salt**

2 **spring onions,**
   finely chopped

10ml/2 tsp **dry sherry**

15ml/1 tbsp **sesame seeds**,
   toasted (see cook's tip)

shredded **spring onion**,
   to garnish

prawn toasts with sesame seeds

method

SERVES 4–6

1 Preheat the oven to 120ºC/250ºF/Gas 1/2. Cut each slice of bread
   into four triangles. Spread out on a baking sheet and bake for
   25 minutes, or until crisp.

2 Meanwhile, put the prawns in a food processor with the water
   chestnuts, egg white, sesame oil and salt. Process until a coarse purée
   is formed.

3 Scrape the mixture into a bowl, stir in the chopped spring onions and
   sherry and marinate for 10 minutes.

4 Remove the toast from the oven and raise the temperature to 200ºC/
   400ºF/Gas 6. Spread the prawn mixture on the toast, sprinkle with
   sesame seeds and bake for 12 minutes. Garnish with spring onion
   and serve hot or warm.

cook's tip
To toast sesame seeds, put them in a dry frying pan and place over
a medium heat until the seeds change colour. Shake the pan constantly
to prevent them from burning.

crab spring rolls
& dipping sauce

CHILLI AND GINGER ADD A **HINT OF HEAT** TO THESE **SENSATIONAL** TREATS. SERVE THEM AS A STARTER OR **SIDE DISH**.

method

SERVES 4–6

1 Heat a wok briefly, then add the groundnut oil and sesame oil. When hot, stir-fry the crushed garlic and chilli for 1 minute. Add the vegetables and ginger and stir-fry for 1 minute more.

2 Drizzle the sherry or rice wine and soy sauce over the vegetables. Allow the mixture to bubble up for 1 minute.

3 Using a slotted spoon, transfer the vegetables to a dish. Set aside until cool, then stir in the crab meat and season with salt and pepper.

4 Soften the spring roll wrappers following the directions on the packet. Place some of the filling on a wrapper, fold over the front edge and the sides and roll up neatly, sealing the edges with a little beaten egg. Repeat with the remaining wrappers and filling.

5 Heat the oil in the wok and fry the spring rolls in batches, turning several times, until brown and crisp. Remove with a slotted spoon, drain on kitchen paper and keep hot while frying the remainder. Serve at once and with the sambal kecap, garnished with lime wedges and coriander.

ingredients

15ml/1 tbsp **groundnut oil**

5ml/1 tsp **sesame oil**

1 **garlic** clove, crushed

1 fresh **red chilli**, seeded and finely sliced

450g/1lb pack fresh stir-fry **vegetables**

2.5cm/1in piece of fresh root **ginger**, grated

15ml/1 tbsp dry **sherry** or Chinese **rice wine**

15ml/1 tbsp **soy sauce**

350g/12oz fresh dressed **crab meat** (brown and white meat)

12 **spring roll wrappers**

1 small **egg**, beaten

oil, for deep frying

salt and freshly ground **black pepper**

Indonesian sambal kecap, to serve

lime wedges and fresh **coriander**, to garnish

cook's tip
Spring roll wrappers are available in many supermarkets as well as Oriental grocers. If you are unable to find them, use filo pastry instead. Keep the wrappers and filled rolls covered with clear film, as they will dry out if exposed to the air.

mussels in black bean sauce

THE LARGE **GREEN-SHELLED** MUSSELS FROM **NEW ZEALAND** ARE **PERFECT** FOR THIS DELICIOUS DISH. BUY THE **COOKED MUSSELS** ON THE HALF SHELL.

ingredients

15ml/1 tbsp **vegetable oil**

2.5cm/1in piece of fresh **root ginger**, finely chopped

2 **garlic** cloves, finely chopped

1 fresh **red chilli**, seeded and chopped

15ml/1 tbsp **black bean sauce**

15ml/1 tbsp **dry sherry**

5ml/1 tsp **caster sugar**

5ml/1 tsp **sesame oil**

10ml/2 tsp **dark soy sauce**

20 cooked New Zealand **green-shelled mussels**

2 **spring onions**, 1 shredded and 1 cut into fine rings

method

SERVES 4–6

1 Heat the vegetable oil in a small frying pan. Fry the ginger, garlic and chilli with the black bean sauce for a few seconds, then add the sherry and caster sugar and cook for 30 seconds more.

2 Remove the sauce from the heat and stir in the sesame oil and soy sauce. Mix thoroughly.

3 Have ready a saucepan with about 5cm/2in of boiling water and a heatproof plate that will fit neatly inside it. Place the mussels in a single layer on the plate. Spoon over the sauce.

4 Sprinkle the spring onions over the mussels, cover the plate tightly with foil and place it in the pan on a metal trivet. Steam over a high heat for about 10 minutes, or until the mussels have heated through. Serve immediately.

cook's tip
Large scallops in their shells can be cooked in the same way. Do not overcook the shellfish.

mini phoenix rolls

THESE **ROLLS** ARE AN **EASY STARTER** AND CAN BE SERVED **HOT** OR **COLD**.

method

SERVES 4

1 Lightly beat the 2 whole eggs with 45ml/3 tbsp of the water. Heat a 20cm/8in omelette pan and brush with a little of the oil. Pour in a quarter of the egg mixture, swirling the pan to coat the base lightly. Cook the omelette until the top is set. Slide it on to a plate and make three more omelettes in the same way.

2 Mix the pork and water chestnuts in a food processor. Add 5ml/1 tsp of the root ginger. Drain the mushrooms, chop the caps roughly and add these to the mixture. Process until smooth.

3 Scrape the pork paste into a bowl. Stir in the egg white, sherry, remaining water, salt and pepper. Mix thoroughly, cover and leave in a cool place for about 15 minutes.

4 Have ready a saucepan with about 5cm/2in boiling water and a large heatproof plate that will fit inside it on a metal trivet. Divide the pork mixture among the omelettes and spread into a large square shape in the centre of each of the omelettes.

5 Bring the sides of each omelette over the filling and roll up from the bottom to the top. Arrange the rolls on the plate. Cover the plate tightly with foil and place it in the pan on the trivet. Steam over a high heat for 15 minutes.

6 Make a dipping sauce by mixing the remaining ginger with the rice vinegar and sugar in a small dish. Cut the rolls diagonally in 1cm/½in slices, garnish with the coriander or flat leaf parsley leaves and serve with the sauce.

ingredients

2 large **eggs**, plus 1 **egg white**
75ml/5 tbsp **cold water**
5ml/1 tsp **vegetable oil**
175g/6oz lean **pork**, diced
75g/3oz/½ cup drained, canned
  water chestnuts
5cm/2in piece of fresh **root**
  ginger, grated
4 dried **Chinese mushrooms**,
  soaked in hot water until soft
15ml/1 tbsp dry **sherry**
1.5ml/¼ tsp **salt**
large pinch of freshly ground
  white pepper
30ml/2 tbsp **rice vinegar**
2.5ml/½ tsp **caster sugar**
fresh **coriander** or **flat leaf**
  parsley, to garnish

> ### cook's tip
> These rolls can be prepared a day in advance and then steamed just before serving.

THIS **PRETTY** DISH IS NOT AS **HOT** AND **FIERY** AS YOU MIGHT EXPECT. DO GIVE IT A TRY.

ingredients

10 fat fresh **green chillies**

115g/4oz lean **pork**, roughly chopped

75g/3oz raw **tiger prawns**, peeled and deveined

15g/½oz/½ cup fresh **coriander** leaves

5ml/1 tsp **cornflour**

10ml/2 tsp dry **sherry**

10ml/2 tsp **soy sauce**

5ml/1 tsp **sesame oil**

2.5ml/½ tsp **salt**

15ml/1 tbsp cold **water**

1 fresh **red** and 1 fresh **green chilli**, seeded and sliced into rings, and cooked **peas**, to garnish

stuffed chillies

method

SERVES 4

1 Cut the chillies in half lengthways, keeping the stalk. Scrape out and discard the seeds and set the chillies aside.

2 Mix together the pork, prawns and coriander leaves in a food processor. Process until smooth. Scrape into a bowl and mix in the cornflour, sherry, soy sauce, sesame oil, salt and water; cover and leave to marinate for 10 minutes.

3 Fill each half chilli with some of the meat mixture. Have ready a saucepan with about 5cm/2in boiling water and a steamer or heatproof plate that will fit inside it on a trivet.

4 Place the stuffed chillies in the steamer or on a plate, meat side up, and cover with a lid or foil. Steam steadily for 15 minutes, or until the meat filling is cooked. Serve immediately, garnished with the chilli rings and peas.

cook's tip
If you prefer a slightly hotter taste, stuff fresh hot red chillies as well as the green ones.

chicken & vegetable bundles

THIS **POPULAR** AND DELICIOUS DIM SUM IS **EXTREMELY EASY** TO PREPARE IN YOUR **OWN KITCHEN**.

ingredients

4 skinless, boneless
   chicken thighs
5ml/1 tsp **cornflour**
10ml/2 tsp **dry sherry**
30ml/2 tbsp **light soy sauce**
2.5ml/1/2 tsp **salt**
large pinch of freshly ground
   white pepper
4 fresh **shiitake mushrooms**
1 small **carrot**
1 small **courgette**
50g/2oz/1/2 cup sliced, drained,
   canned **bamboo shoots**
1 **leek**, trimmed
1.5ml/1/4 tsp **sesame oil**

method

SERVES 4

1 Remove any fat from the chicken thighs and cut each lengthways into eight strips. Place the strips in a bowl.

2 Add the cornflour, sherry and half the soy sauce to the chicken. Stir in the salt and pepper and mix well. Cover and marinate for 10 minutes.

3 Remove and discard the mushroom stalks, then cut each mushroom cap in half (or in slices if very large). Cut the carrot and courgette into eight batons, each about 5cm/2in long, then mix the mushroom halves and bamboo shoots together.

4 Bring a small saucepan of water to the boil. Add the leek and blanch until soft. Drain thoroughly, then slit the leek down its length. Separate each layer to give eight long strips.

5 Divide the marinated chicken into eight portions. Do the same with the vegetables. Wrap each strip of leek around a portion of chicken and vegetables to make eight neat bundles. Have ready a saucepan with about 5cm/2in boiling water and a steamer or a heatproof plate that will fit inside it on a metal trivet.

6 Place the chicken and vegetable bundles in the steamer or on the plate. Place in the pan, cover and steam over a high heat for 12–15 minutes, or until the filling is cooked. Meanwhile, mix the remaining soy sauce with the sesame oil and use as a sauce for the bundles.

fish & shellfish

ingredients

300ml/½ pint/1¼ cups
   fish stock
350g/12oz raw **tiger prawns**,
   peeled and deveined
15ml/1 tbsp **vegetable oil**
1 **garlic** clove, finely chopped
225g/8oz/2 cups **mangetouts**
1.5ml/¼ tsp **salt**
15ml/1 tbsp dry **sherry**
15ml/1 tbsp **oyster sauce**
5ml/1 tsp **cornflour**
5ml/1 tsp **caster sugar**
15ml/1 tbsp **water**
1.5ml/¼ tsp **sesame oil**

stir-fried prawns with mangetouts

PRAWNS AND **MANGETOUTS** MAKE A PRETTY DISH, WHICH NEEDS NO **EMBELLISHMENT**.

method

SERVES 4

1 Bring the fish stock to the boil in a frying pan. Add the prawns. Cook gently for 2 minutes, until the prawns have turned pink, then drain and set aside.

2 Heat the vegetable oil in a frying pan or wok. Add the chopped garlic and cook for a few seconds, then add the mangetouts. Sprinkle with the salt. Stir-fry for 1 minute.

3 Add the prawns and sherry to the pan or wok. Stir-fry for a few seconds, then add the oyster sauce.

4 Mix the cornflour and sugar to a paste with the water. Add the mixture to the pan and cook, stirring constantly, until the sauce thickens slightly. Drizzle with the sesame oil and serve.

grey mullet with pork

THIS UNUSUAL **COMBINATION** MAKES A
SPECTACULAR MAIN DISH WITH VERY
LITTLE EFFORT.

method

SERVES 4

1 Make four diagonal cuts on either side of the fish and rub with a little salt. Place the fish on a large, shallow, heatproof serving dish.

2 Cut the pork into thin strips. Place in a bowl. Drain the soaked mushrooms, remove and discard the stalks and slice the caps thinly.

3 Add the mushrooms to the pork, with the cornflour and half the soy sauce. Stir in 5ml/1 tsp of the oil and a generous grinding of black pepper. Arrange the pork mixture along the length of the fish. Scatter the ginger shreds over the top.

4 Cover the fish loosely with foil. Have ready a large saucepan or roasting tin with about 5cm/2in boiling water, which is big enough to fit the heatproof dish inside it on a metal trivet. Place the dish in the pan or roasting tin, cover and steam over a high heat for 15 minutes.

5 Test the fish by pressing the flesh gently. If it comes away from the bone with a slight resistance, the fish is cooked. Carefully pour away any excess liquid from the dish

6 Heat the remaining oil in a small pan. When it is hot, fry the shredded spring onion for a few seconds then pour it over the fish, taking great care as it will splatter. Drizzle with the remaining soy sauce, garnish with sliced spring onion and serve immediately with rice.

> ### cook's tip
> If the fish is too big to fit into the steamer whole, simply cut it
> in half for cooking, then reassemble it to serve.

ingredients

1 **grey mullet**, about 900g/2lb,
  gutted and cleaned
50g/2oz lean **pork**
3 dried **Chinese mushrooms**,
  soaked in hot water until soft
2.5ml/½ tsp **cornflour**
30ml/2 tbsp **light soy sauce**
15ml/1 tbsp **vegetable oil**
15ml/1 tbsp finely shredded fresh
  root ginger
15ml/1 tbsp shredded
  spring onion
salt and freshly ground
  black pepper
sliced **spring onion**, to garnish
rice, to serve

asparagus with crab meat sauce

THE **SUBTLE** FLAVOUR OF FRESH ASPARAGUS IS ENHANCED BY THE EQUALLY **DELICATE** TASTE OF **CRAB** IN THIS **CLASSIC DISH**.

method

SERVES 4

1 Bring a large pan of lightly salted water to the boil. Poach the asparagus for about 5 minutes, until just crisp-tender. Drain well and keep hot in a shallow serving dish.

2 Heat the oil in a frying pan or wok. Cook the ginger and garlic for 1 minute to release their flavour, then lift them out with a slotted spoon and discard them.

3 Add the crab meat, sherry and milk to the flavoured oil and cook, stirring frequently, for 2 minutes.

4 In a small bowl, mix the cornflour to a paste with the water and add to the pan. Cook, stirring constantly, until the sauce is thick and creamy. Season to taste with salt and pepper, spoon over the asparagus, garnish with shreds of spring onion and serve.

ingredients

450g/1lb **asparagus**, trimmed
15ml/1 tbsp **vegetable oil**
4 thin slices of fresh **root ginger**
2 **garlic** cloves, finely chopped
115g/4oz/2/3 cup fresh or thawed
　　frozen white **crab meat**
5ml/1 tsp dry **sherry**
150ml/1/4 pint/2/3 cup **milk**
15ml/1 tbsp **cornflour**
45ml/3 tbsp cold **water**
salt and freshly ground
　　white pepper
1 **spring onion**, thinly shredded,
　　to garnish

THIS TASTY,
COLOURFUL SALAD
IS A **REFRESHING**
WAY OF SERVING
SUCCULENT SQUID

ingredients

450g/1lb **squid**

300ml/1/2 pint/1 1/4 cups
fish stock

175g/6oz **green beans**, trimmed
and halved

45ml/3 tbsp fresh
coriander leaves

10ml/2 tsp **caster sugar**

30ml/2 tbsp **rice vinegar**

5ml/1 tsp **sesame oil**

15ml/1 tbsp **light soy sauce**

15ml/1 tbsp **vegetable oil**

2 **garlic** cloves, finely chopped

10ml/2 tsp finely chopped fresh
root ginger

1 fresh **chilli**, seeded and
chopped

salt, to taste

spicy squid salad

method

SERVES 4

1 Prepare the squid. Holding the body in one hand, gently pull away the head and tentacles. Discard the head. Trim and reserve the tentacles. Remove the transparent "quill" from inside the body of the squid and peel off the purplish skin on the outside.

2 Cut the body of the squid open lengthways and wash thoroughly. Score criss-cross patterns on the inside, taking care not to cut through the squid, then cut into 7.5 x 5cm/3 x 2in pieces.

3 Bring the fish stock to the boil in a wok or saucepan. Add all the squid pieces, then lower the heat and cook for about 2 minutes, until they are tender and have curled. Drain.

4 In a separate pan of lightly salted boiling water, cook the beans until crisp-tender. Drain, refresh under cold water, then drain again. Mix the squid and beans in a serving bowl.

5 In a bowl or jug, mix the coriander leaves, sugar, rice vinegar, sesame oil and soy sauce. Pour the mixture over the squid and beans.

6 Heat the vegetable oil in a wok or small pan until very hot. Stir-fry the garlic, ginger and chilli for a few seconds, then pour the dressing over the squid mixture. Toss gently and leave for at least 5 minutes. Add salt to taste and serve warm or cold.

---

cook's tip
If you hold your knife at an angle when scoring the squid there is less of a risk of cutting right through it.

three sea flavours stir-fry

THIS **DELECTABLE** SEAFOOD COMBINATION IS **ENHANCED** BY THE USE OF **FRESH ROOT GINGER** AND SPRING ONIONS.

ingredients

4 large **scallops**, with the corals
225g/8oz firm **white fish** fillet,
  such as monkfish or cod
115g/4oz raw **tiger prawns**
300ml/1/2 pint/11/4 cups
  fish stock
15ml/1 tbsp **vegetable oil**
2 **garlic** cloves, coarsely chopped
5cm/2in piece of fresh **root**
  ginger, thinly sliced
8 **spring onions**, cut into
  4cm/11/2in pieces
30ml/2 tbsp **dry white wine**
5ml/1 tsp **cornflour**
15ml/1 tbsp **cold water**
salt and freshly ground
  white pepper
noodles or **rice**, to serve

---

cook's tip
Do not overcook the seafood or
it will become rubbery.

---

method

SERVES 4

1 Separate the corals and slice each scallop in half horizontally. Cut the fish fillet into bite-size chunks. Peel and devein the prawns.

2 Bring the fish stock to the boil in a saucepan. Add the seafood, lower the heat and poach gently for 1–2 minutes, until the fish, scallops and corals are just firm and the prawns have turned pink. Drain the seafood, reserving about 60ml/4 tbsp of the stock.

3 Heat the oil in a frying pan or wok over a high heat until very hot. Stir-fry the garlic, ginger and spring onions for a few seconds.

4 Add the seafood and wine. Stir-fry for 1 minute, then add the reserved stock and simmer for 2 minutes.

5 Mix the cornflour to a paste with the water. Add the mixture to the pan or wok and cook, stirring gently just until the sauce thickens.

6 Season the stir-fry with salt and pepper to taste. Serve at once, with noodles or rice.

monkfish & scallop skewers

USING **LEMON GRASS** STALKS AS SKEWERS IMBUES THE SEAFOOD WITH A **SUBTLE CITRUS** FLAVOUR.

method

SERVES 4

1 Remove any membrane from the monkfish fillet, then cut it into 16 large chunks.

ingredients

450g/1lb **monkfish** fillet

8 **lemon grass** stalks

30ml/2 tbsp fresh **lemon juice**

15ml/1 tbsp **olive oil**

15ml/1 tbsp finely chopped
   fresh **coriander**

2.5ml/½ tsp **salt**

large pinch of freshly ground
   black pepper

12 large **scallops**,
   halved crossways

fresh **coriander** leaves, to garnish

rice, to serve

variation
Raw tiger prawns and salmon
make excellent alternative
ingredients for the skewers, with
or without the monkfish.

2 Remove the outer leaves from the lemon grass to leave thin rigid stalks. Chop the tender parts of the lemon grass leaves finely and place in a bowl. Stir in the lemon juice, oil, chopped coriander, salt and pepper.

3 Thread the fish and scallop chunks alternately on the 8 lemon grass stalks. Arrange the skewers of fish and shellfish in a shallow dish and pour over the marinade.

4 Cover and leave in a cool place for at least 1 hour, turning occasionally. Transfer the skewers to a heatproof dish or bamboo steamer, cover and steam over boiling water for 10 minutes, until just cooked. Garnish with coriander and serve with rice and the cooking juice poured over.

THE SLIGHTLY CHEWY SQUID **CONTRASTS BEAUTIFULLY** WITH THE **CRISP CRUNCH** OF THE BROCCOLI TO GIVE THIS DISH THE **PERFECT COMBINATION** OF TEXTURES THAT IS SO **HIGHLY PRIZED** BY THE CHINESE.

ingredients

300ml/½ pint/1¼ cups
  fish stock
350g/12oz prepared **squid**,
  cut into large pieces
225g/8oz **broccoli**
15ml/1 tbsp **vegetable oil**
2 **garlic** cloves, finely chopped
15ml/1 tbsp **dry sherry**
10ml/2 tsp **cornflour**
2.5ml/½ tsp **caster sugar**
45ml/3 tbsp **water**
15ml/1 tbsp **oyster sauce**
2.5ml/½ tsp **sesame oil**
noodles, to serve

squid with broccoli

method

SERVES 4

1 Bring the fish stock to the boil in a wok or saucepan. Cook the squid pieces for 2 minutes, until they are tender and have curled. Drain and set aside.

2 Trim the broccoli and cut into small florets. Cook in a saucepan of boiling water for 2 minutes until crisp-tender. Drain thoroughly.

3 Heat the vegetable oil in a wok or frying pan. Stir-fry the garlic for a few seconds, then add the squid, broccoli and sherry. Stir-fry for about 2 minutes.

4 Mix the cornflour and sugar to a paste with the water. Stir the mixture into the wok or pan, with the oyster sauce. Cook, stirring, until the sauce thickens slightly. Just before serving, stir in the sesame oil. Serve with noodles.

gong boa prawns

A PLEASANTLY SPICY **SWEET-&-SOUR** DISH THAT TAKES ONLY **MINUTES** TO MAKE.

ingredients

350g/12oz raw **tiger prawns**
1/2 **cucumber**, about 75g/3oz
300ml/1/2 pint/11/4 cups
  fish stock
15ml/1 tbsp **vegetable oil**
2.5ml/1/2 tsp crushed
  dried **chillies**
1/2 **green pepper**, seeded and
  cut into 2.5cm/1in strips
1 small **carrot**, thinly sliced
30ml/2 tbsp **tomato ketchup**
45ml/3 tbsp **rice vinegar**
15ml/1 tbsp **caster sugar**
150ml/1/4 pint/2/3 cup
  vegetable stock
50g/2oz/1/2 cup drained canned
  pineapple chunks
10ml/2 tsp **cornflour**
15ml/1 tbsp **water**
salt

cook's tip
If you do not have any fish stock, make a quick stock by boiling the prawn shells with an onion and a carrot in 475ml/3/4 pint/2 cups water for 10 minutes. Strain and use as indicated in the recipe.

method

SERVES 4

1 Peel and devein the prawns. Rub them gently with 2.5ml/1/2 tsp salt, leave them for a few minutes and then wash and dry thoroughly.

2 Using a narrow peeler or canelle knife, pare strips of skin off the cucumber to give a stripy effect. Cut the cucumber in half lengthways and scoop out the seeds with a teaspoon. Cut the flesh into 5mm/1/4in crescents.

3 Bring the fish stock to the boil in a saucepan. Add the prawns, lower the heat and poach the prawns for about 2 minutes, until they turn pink, then drain and set aside.

4 Heat the oil in a frying pan or wok over a high heat. Fry the chillies for a few seconds, then add the pepper strips and carrot slices and stir-fry for 1 minute.

5 Mix together the tomato ketchup, vinegar, sugar and vegetable stock, with 1.5ml/1/4 tsp salt. Pour the mixture into the pan and cook for 3 minutes more.

6 Add the prawns, cucumber and pineapple and cook for 2 minutes more. Mix the cornflour to a paste with the water. Add the mixture to the pan and cook, stirring constantly, until the sauce thickens. Serve at once.

variation
You can omit the dried chillies if you like, or increase the quantity for a much spicier dish.

poultry

chicken with lemon sauce

SUCCULENT CHICKEN WITH A **REFRESHING** LEMONY SAUCE AND **JUST** A **HINT** OF LIME IS A **SURE WINNER**.

method

SERVES 4

1 Arrange the chicken breasts in a single layer in a shallow bowl. Mix the sesame oil with the sherry and add 2.5ml/1/2 tsp salt and 1.5ml/1/4 tsp pepper. Pour over the chicken, cover and marinate for 15 minutes.

2 Mix together the egg white and cornflour. Add the mixture to the chicken and turn the chicken with tongs until thoroughly coated. Heat the vegetable oil in a frying pan or wok and fry the chicken fillets for about 15 minutes, until they are golden brown on both sides.

3 Meanwhile, make the sauce. Combine all the ingredients in a small pan. Add 1.5ml/1/4 tsp salt. Bring to the boil over a low heat, stirring constantly, until the sauce is smooth and has thickened slightly.

4 Cut the chicken into pieces and arrange on a warm serving plate. Pour the sauce over, garnish with the coriander leaves, spring onions and lemon wedges and serve.

ingredients

4 small skinless **chicken** breast fillets
5ml/1 tsp **sesame oil**
15ml/1 tbsp **dry sherry**
salt and freshly ground **white pepper**
1 **egg white**, lightly beaten
30ml/2 tbsp **cornflour**
15ml/1 tbsp **vegetable oil**
chopped **coriander** leaves and **spring onions** and **lemon wedges**, to garnish

For the sauce
45ml/3 tbsp fresh **lemon juice**
30ml/2 tbsp **lime cordial**
45ml/3 tbsp **caster sugar**
10ml/2 tsp **cornflour**
90ml/6 tbsp **water**

ingredients

350g/12oz skinless **chicken**
   breast fillets
20ml/4 tsp **vegetable oil**
300ml/½ pint/1¼ cups **chicken**
   stock
75g/3oz/¾ cup drained, canned
   straw mushrooms
50g/2oz/½ cup sliced, drained,
   canned **bamboo shoots**
50g/2oz/⅓ cup drained, canned
   water chestnuts, sliced
1 small **carrot**, sliced
50g/2oz/½ cup **mangetouts**
15ml/1 tbsp dry **sherry**
15ml/1 tbsp **oyster sauce**
5ml/1 tsp **caster sugar**
5ml/1 tsp **cornflour**
15ml/1 tbsp **cold water**
salt and freshly ground
   white pepper

chicken with mixed vegetables

A **RIOT** OF **COLOUR**, THIS FLAVOURSOME
DISH HAS PLENTY OF **CONTRASTS** IN TERMS
OF **TEXTURE** AND **TASTE**.

method

SERVES 4

1 Put the chicken in a shallow bowl. Add 5ml/1 tsp of the oil, 1.5ml/
¼ tsp salt and a pinch of pepper. Cover and set aside for 10 minutes
in a cool place.

2 Bring the stock to the boil in a saucepan. Add the chicken and cook
for 12 minutes, or until tender. Drain and slice, reserving 75ml/5 tbsp
of the stock.

3 Heat the remaining oil in a frying pan or wok, add all the vegetables
and stir-fry for 2 minutes. Stir in the sherry, oyster sauce, caster sugar
and reserved stock. Add the chicken to the pan and cook for
2 minutes more.

4 Mix the cornflour to a paste with the water. Add the mixture to the pan
and cook, stirring, until the sauce thickens slightly. Season to taste
with salt and pepper and serve immediately.

salt-baked chicken

THIS IS A **FABULOUS** WAY OF COOKING CHICKEN. THE DELICIOUS, **SUCCULENT** JUICES ARE **SEALED** INSIDE THE **SALT CRUST**, YET THE FLAVOUR ISN'T SALTY.

ingredients

1.5kg/3–3½lb corn-fed **chicken**

1.5ml/¼ tsp fine **sea salt**

2.25kg/5lb coarse **rock salt**

15ml/1 tbsp **vegetable oil**

2.5cm/1in piece fresh **root ginger**, finely chopped

4 **spring onions**, cut into fine rings

boiled rice, garnished with shredded **spring onions**, to serve

cook's tips

The dry salt around the top of the chicken can be used again, but the salt from under the bird should be thrown away, as this will have absorbed fat and cooking juices. To reduce the fat content, remove and discard the skin from the chicken before eating.

method

SERVES 4

1 Rinse the chicken. Pat it dry, both inside and out, with kitchen paper, then rub the inside with the sea salt.

2 Place four pieces of damp kitchen paper on the bottom of a heavy-based frying pan or wok just large enough to hold the chicken.

3 Sprinkle a layer of rock salt over the kitchen paper, about 1cm/½in thick. Place the chicken on top of the salt.

4 Pour the remaining salt over the chicken until it is completely covered. Dampen six more pieces of kitchen paper and place these around the rim of the pan or wok. Cover with a tight-fitting lid. Put the pan or wok over a high heat for 10 minutes, or until it gives off a slightly smoky smell.

5 Immediately reduce the heat to medium and continue to cook the chicken for 30 minutes without lifting the lid. After 30 minutes, turn off the heat and leave for a further 10 minutes before carefully lifting the chicken out of the salt. Brush off any salt still clinging to the chicken and allow the bird to cool for 20 minutes before cutting it into serving-size pieces.

6 Heat the oil in a small saucepan until very hot. Add the ginger and spring onions and fry for a few seconds, then pour into a heatproof bowl and use as a dipping sauce for the chicken. Serve the chicken with boiled rice, garnished with shredded spring onions.

ingredients

350g/12oz skinless **chicken**
   breast fillets
1.5ml/¼ tsp **salt**
pinch of freshly ground
   white pepper
15ml/1 tbsp dry **sherry**
300ml/½ pint/1¼ cups **chicken**
   stock
15ml/1 tbsp **vegetable oil**
1 **garlic** clove, finely chopped
1 small **carrot**, cut into cubes
½ **cucumber**, about 75g/3oz,
   cut into 1cm/½in cubes
50g/2oz/½ cup drained canned
   bamboo shoots, cut into
   1cm/½in cubes
5ml/1 tsp **cornflour**
15ml/1 tbsp light **soy sauce**
5ml/1 tsp **caster sugar**
25g/1oz/¼ cup dry-roasted
   cashew nuts
2.5ml/½ tsp **sesame oil**
noodles, to serve

chicken
with cashew nuts

AN **ALL-TIME** FAVOURITE, THIS **CLASSIC**
DISH IS DELIGHTFULLY **QUICK** AND **EASY**
TO PREPARE.

method
SERVES 4

1 Cut the chicken into 2cm/¾in cubes. Place the cubes in a bowl, stir
in the salt, pepper and sherry, cover and marinate for 15 minutes.

2 Bring the stock to the boil in a large saucepan. Add the chicken and
cook, stirring, for 3 minutes. Drain, reserving 90ml/6 tbsp of the
stock, and set aside.

3 Heat the vegetable oil in a frying pan until very hot, add the garlic and
stir-fry for a few seconds. Add the carrot, cucumber and bamboo
shoots and continue to stir-fry over a medium heat for 2 minutes.

4 Stir in the chicken and reserved stock. Mix the cornflour with the soy
sauce and sugar and add the mixture to the pan. Cook, stirring, until
the sauce thickens slightly. Finally, add the cashew nuts and sesame
oil. Toss to mix thoroughly, then serve with noodles.

---

cook's tip
Peanuts or almonds can be used in this recipe instead of
cashews if you prefer.

---

bang bang chicken

WHAT A **DESCRIPTIVE** NAME THIS FAMOUS DISH HAS. THE SAUCE GETS ITS **AUTHENTIC FLAVOUR** FROM **SESAME PASTE**, ALTHOUGH PEANUT BUTTER CAN BE USED INSTEAD.

method

SERVES 4

1 Place the chicken breasts in a saucepan. Just cover with water, add the onion and garlic and bring to the boil. Skim the surface and stir in salt and pepper to taste. Cover and cook for 25 minutes, until the chicken is just tender. Drain, reserving the stock.

2 Make the sauce by mixing the sesame paste with 45ml/3 tbsp of the stock. Add the soy sauce, vinegar, spring onions, garlic, ginger and peppercorns. Stir in sugar to taste.

3 Make the chilli oil by gently heating the oil and chilli powder together until foaming. Simmer for 2 minutes, cool then strain off the red-coloured oil. Discard the sediment.

4 Spread out the cucumber batons on a platter. Cut the chicken into pieces about the same size as the cucumber and arrange on top. Pour over the sauce, drizzle on the chilli oil and serve. Guests will toss their own helpings before eating.

> ### cook's tip
> Crunchy peanut butter can be used instead of sesame paste, if preferred. Mix 45ml/3 tbsp with 30ml/2 tbsp sesame oil and proceed as in step 2.

ingredients

3 skinless, boneless **chicken** breasts, about 450g/1lb
1 small **onion**, halved
1 **garlic** clove, crushed
salt and freshly ground **black pepper**
1 large **cucumber**, peeled, seeded and cut into batons, to serve

For the sauce
45ml/3 tbsp **sesame paste**
15ml/1 tbsp light **soy sauce**
15ml/1 tbsp wine **vinegar**
2 **spring onions**, finely chopped
2 **garlic** cloves, crushed
1cm/½in piece of fresh **root ginger**, grated
15ml/1 tbsp **Szechuan peppercorns**, dry-fried and crushed
5ml/1 tsp light **brown sugar**

For the chilli oil
60ml/4 tbsp **groundnut oil**
5ml/1 tsp **chilli powder**

anita wong's duck

THE CHINESE ARE **PASSIONATELY** FOND OF DUCK AND REGARD IT AS AN **ESSENTIAL** ON **CELEBRATORY** OCCASIONS. DUCK DENOTES **MARITAL HARMONY**.

method

SERVES 4–6

1 Use the giblets to make a duck stock. Blot the surface with kitchen paper to remove excess fat, then strain. Reserve 450ml/¾ pint/1¾ cups.

2 Heat the oil in a deep frying pan. Fry the garlic without browning, then add the duck. Turn frequently until the outside is slightly brown. Lift the duck on to a plate.

3 Add the ginger to the pan, then stir in the bean paste. Cook for 1 minute, then add both soy sauces, the sugar and the five-spice powder. Return the duck to the pan and fry until the outside is coated. Add the star anise and stock or water, and season to taste. Cover and cook over a gentle heat for 2–2½ hours or until tender, stirring occasionally. Skim or blot the surface to remove the excess fat or oil, then leave the duck in the sauce to cool.

4 Cut the duck into serving portions and pour over the sauce. Garnish with spring onion curls and serve cold.

ingredients

1 **duck** with giblets, about 2.25kg/5–5¼lb
60ml/4 tbsp **vegetable oil**
2 **garlic cloves**, chopped
2.5cm/1in piece **fresh root ginger**, thinly sliced
45ml/3 tbsp **bean paste**
30ml/2 tbsp **light soy sauce**
15ml/1 tbsp **dark soy sauce**
15ml/1 tbsp **sugar**
2.5ml/½ tsp **five-spice powder**
3 points **star anise**
450ml/¾ pint/1¾ cups **duck stock** or **water**, (see step 1)
salt
spring onion curls, to garnish

cook's tip
Store any leftover sauce in a jar in the fridge for a few days. Use as a marinade for steak or chicken drumsticks, or stir into gravy for extra flavour.

ingredients

15ml/1 tbsp dry **sherry**

15ml/1 tbsp **dark soy sauce**

2 small skinless **duck** breasts

15ml/1 tbsp **vegetable oil**

2 **garlic** cloves, finely chopped

1 small **onion**, sliced

1 **red pepper**, seeded and cut
    into 2.5cm/1in squares

75g/3oz/1/2 cup drained, canned
    pineapple chunks

90ml/6 tbsp **pineapple** juice

15ml/1 tbsp **rice vinegar**

5ml/1 tsp **cornflour**

15ml/1 tbsp cold **water**

5ml/1 tsp **sesame oil**

salt and freshly ground
    white pepper

1 **spring onion**, shredded,
    to garnish

duck with pineapple

DUCK AND PINEAPPLE IS A FAVOURITE
COMBINATION, BUT THE FRUIT MUST NOT
BE ALLOWED TO DOMINATE. HERE THE
PROPORTIONS ARE **PERFECT** AND THE
DISH HAS A WONDERFULLY **SUBTLE** SWEET-
SOUR FLAVOUR.

method

SERVES 4

1 Mix together the sherry and soy sauce. Stir in 2.5ml/1/2 tsp salt and
   1.5ml/1/4 tsp pepper. Put the duck breasts in a bowl and add the
   marinade. Cover and leave in a cool place for 1 hour.

2 Drain the duck breasts and place them on a rack in a grill pan. Grill
   under a medium to high heat for 10 minutes on each side. Allow to
   cool for 10 minutes, then cut into bite-size pieces.

3 Heat the vegetable oil in a frying pan or wok and stir-fry the garlic and
   onion for 1 minute. Add the red pepper, pineapple chunks, duck,
   pineapple juice and vinegar and stir-fry for 2 minutes.

4 Mix the cornflour to a paste with the water. Add the mixture to the pan
   with 1.5ml/1/4 tsp salt. Cook, stirring until the sauce thickens. Stir in
   the sesame oil and serve at once, garnished with spring onion shreds.

duck with pancakes

ingredients

15ml/1 tbsp clear **honey**

1.5ml/1/4 tsp Chinese **five spice powder**

1 **garlic** clove, finely chopped

15ml/1 tbsp **hoisin sauce**

2.5ml/1/2 tsp **salt**

a large pinch of freshly ground **white pepper**

2 small skinless **duck** breasts

1/2 **cucumber**

10 **spring onions**

3 **Chinese leaves**

12 **Chinese pancakes** (see cook's tip)

For the sauce

5ml/1 tsp **vegetable oil**

2 **garlic** cloves, chopped

2 **spring onions**, chopped

1cm/1/2in piece of fresh **root ginger**, bruised

60ml/4 tbsp **hoisin sauce**

15ml/1 tbsp **dry sherry**

15ml/1 tbsp **water**

2.5ml/1/2 tsp **sesame oil**

cook's tip

Chinese pancakes can be bought frozen from Chinese supermarkets. Leave them to thaw before steaming.

CONSIDERABLY LOWER IN FAT THAN TRADITIONAL **PEKING DUCK**, AND JUST AS DELICIOUS. GUESTS SPREAD THEIR **PANCAKES** WITH SAUCE, ADD DUCK AND VEGETABLES, THEN **ROLL THEM UP**.

method

SERVES 4

1 Mix the honey, five spice powder, garlic, hoisin sauce, salt and pepper in a shallow dish large enough to hold the duck breasts side by side. Add the duck breasts, turning them in the marinade. Cover and leave in a cool place to marinate for 2 hours.

2 Cut the cucumber in half lengthways. Using a teaspoon scrape out and discard the seeds. Cut the flesh into thin batons 5cm/2in long.

3 Cut off and discard the green tops from the spring onions. Finely shred the white parts and place on a serving plate with the cucumber batons.

4 Make the sauce. Heat the oil in a small saucepan and gently fry the garlic for a few seconds without browning. Add the spring onions, ginger, hoisin sauce, sherry and water. Cook gently for 5 minutes, stirring often, then strain and mix with the sesame oil.

5 Remove the duck breasts from the marinade and drain them well. Place the duck breasts on a rack over a grill pan. Grill under a medium to high heat for 8–10 minutes on each side. Allow to cool for 5 minutes before cutting into thin slices. Arrange on a serving platter, cover and keep warm.

6 Line a steamer with the Chinese leaves and place the pancakes on top. Have ready a large pan with 5cm/2in boiling water. Cover the steamer and place on a trivet in the pan. Steam over a high heat for 2 minutes, or until the pancakes are hot. Serve at once with the duck, cucumber, spring onions and sauce.

pork & beef

sticky pork ribs

A DELICIOUS DISH WHICH HAS TO BE **EATEN** WITH THE **FINGERS** TO BE ENJOYED FULLY.

method

SERVES 4

1 Combine the caster sugar, five-spice powder, hoisin sauce, yellow bean sauce, garlic, cornflour and salt in a bowl, then mix together well.

2 Place the pork ribs in an ovenproof dish and pour the marinade over. Mix thoroughly, cover and leave in a cool place for 1 hour.

ingredients

30ml/2 tbsp **caster sugar**
2.5ml/½ tsp Chinese **five-spice powder**
45ml/3 tbsp **hoisin sauce**
30ml/2 tbsp **yellow bean sauce**
3 **garlic** cloves, finely chopped
15ml/1 tbsp **cornflour**
2.5ml/½ tsp **salt**
16 **pork ribs**
chives and sliced **spring onion**, to garnish
salad or **rice**, to serve

3 Preheat the oven to 180ºC/350ºF/Gas 4. Cover the dish tightly with foil and bake the pork ribs for 40 minutes. Baste the ribs from time to time with the cooking juices.

4 Remove the foil, baste the ribs and continue to cook for 20 minutes, until glossy and brown. Garnish with chives and spring onion and serve with a salad or rice.

---

cook's tip

These ribs barbecue well. Bake as described in step 3, then transfer them to the barbecue to finish cooking. The sauce coating makes the ribs liable to burn, so watch them closely.

ingredients

15ml/1 tbsp **vegetable oil**

15ml/1 tbsp **hoisin sauce**

15ml/1 tbsp **yellow
    bean sauce**

1.5ml/¼ tsp Chinese **five-
    spice powder**

2.5ml/½ tsp **cornflour**

15ml/1 tbsp **caster sugar**

1.5ml/¼ tsp **salt**

1.5ml/¼ tsp freshly ground
    white pepper

450g/1lb **pork fillet**, trimmed

10ml/2 tsp clear **honey**

shredded **spring onion**,
    to garnish

rice, to serve

char-siu pork

MARINATED PORK, ROASTED AND GLAZED
WITH HONEY, IS SIMPLY IRRESISTIBLE ON
ITS OWN AND CAN ALSO BE USED AS THE
BASIS FOR **SALADS** OR **STIR-FRIES**.

method

SERVES 4

1 Mix the oil, sauces, five spice powder, cornflour, sugar and seasoning
   in a shallow dish. Add the pork and coat it with the mixture. Cover and
   chill for 4 hours or overnight.

2 Preheat the oven to 190°C/375°F/Gas 5. Drain the pork and place it
   on a wire rack over a deep roasting tin. Roast for 40 minutes, turning
   the pork over from time to time.

3 Check that the pork is cooked by inserting a skewer or fork into the
   meat; the juices should run clear. If they are still tinged with pink,
   roast the pork for 5–10 minutes more.

4 Remove the pork from the oven and brush it with the honey. Allow to
   cool for 10 minutes before cutting into thin slices. Garnish with spring
   onion and serve hot or cold with rice.

sweet-&-sour pork

AN **IRRESISTIBLY EASY** VERSION OF THIS POPULAR, **CLASSIC** CHINESE DISH.

ingredients

15ml/1 tbsp **dry sherry**
350g/12oz lean **pork** steaks
15ml/1 tbsp **vegetable oil**
1 **garlic** clove, finely chopped
1/2 **onion**, diced
1 small **green pepper**, seeded
    and cut into 2.5cm/1in squares
1 small **carrot**, sliced
75g/3oz/1/2 cup drained, canned
    pineapple chunks
30ml/2 tbsp **malt vinegar**
45ml/3 tbsp **tomato ketchup**
150ml/1/4 pint/2/3 cup
    pineapple juice
10ml/2 tsp **caster sugar**
10ml/2 tsp **cornflour**
15ml/1 tbsp **water**
salt and freshly ground
    black pepper
rice, to serve

cook's tip
This is a great way of giving leftover pork from the Sunday roast a new lease of life. Cut into bite-size pieces and proceed from step 3.

method

SERVES 4

1 Mix the sherry, 2.5ml/1/2 tsp salt and a large pinch of pepper in a shallow dish. Add the pork, turn to coat, then cover and leave to marinate in a cool place for 15 minutes.

2 Drain the pork steaks and place them on a rack over a grill pan. Grill under a high heat for 5 minutes on each side, or until cooked, then remove and leave to cool. Cut the cooked pork into bite-size pieces.

3 Heat the oil in a frying pan or wok until very hot. Stir-fry the garlic and onion for a few seconds, then add the green pepper and carrot and stir-fry for 1 minute.

4 Stir in the pineapple chunks, vinegar, ketchup, pineapple juice and caster sugar. Bring to the boil, lower the heat and simmer for 3 minutes.

5 Add the cooked pork to the vegetable mixture and cook for about 2 minutes.

6 Mix the cornflour to a paste with the water. Add the mixture to the pan or wok and cook, stirring, until slightly thickened. Serve with rice.

beef in oyster sauce

THE **OYSTER SAUCE** GIVES THE BEEF **EXTRA RICHNESS** AND **DEPTH** OF FLAVOUR. TO COMPLETE THE DISH, ALL YOU NEED IS PLAIN BOILED **RICE** OR **NOODLES**.

ingredients

350g/12oz rump **steak**, trimmed

15ml/1 tbsp **vegetable oil**

300ml/½ pint/1¼ cups
  beef stock

2 **garlic** cloves, finely chopped

1 small **carrot**, thinly sliced

3 **celery** sticks, sliced

15ml/1 tbsp **dry sherry**

5ml/1 tsp **caster sugar**

45ml/3 tbsp **oyster sauce**

5ml/1 tsp **cornflour**

15ml/1 tbsp **water**

4 **spring onions**, cut into
  2.5cm/1in lengths

freshly ground **white pepper**

rice or **noodles**, to serve

method

SERVES 4

1 Slice the beef thinly. Place the slices in a bowl, add 5ml/1 tsp of the vegetable oil and stir to coat.

2 Bring the stock to the boil in a large saucepan. Add the beef and cook, stirring, for 2 minutes. Drain, reserving 45ml/3 tbsp of the stock, and set aside.

3 Heat the remaining oil in a frying pan or wok. Stir-fry the garlic for a few seconds, then add the carrot and celery and stir-fry for 2 minutes.

4 Stir in the sherry, caster sugar, oyster sauce and a large pinch of pepper. Add the beef to the pan with the reserved stock. Simmer for 2 minutes.

5 Mix the cornflour to a paste with the water. Add the mixture to the pan and cook, stirring, until thickened.

6 Stir in the spring onions, mixing well, then serve at once, with boiled rice or noodles.

variation

To increase the number of servings without adding any extra beef, add more vegetables, such as peppers, mangetouts, water chestnuts, baby corn cobs and mushrooms.

beef with peppers & black bean sauce

A **SPICY**, **RICH** DISH WITH THE **DISTINCTIVE** FLAVOUR OF **BLACK BEAN** SAUCE.

method

SERVES 4

1 Place the prepared beef in a large bowl. Add 5ml/1 tsp of the vegetable oil and stir well to coat.

2 Bring the stock to the boil in a saucepan. Add the beef and cook for 2 minutes, stirring constantly to prevent the slices from sticking together. Drain the beef and set aside.

3 Heat the remaining oil in a frying pan or wok. Stir-fry the garlic, ginger and chilli with the black bean sauce for a few seconds. Add the pepper squares and a little water. Cook for about 2 minutes more, then stir in the sherry. Add the beef slices to the pan and spoon the sauce over.

4 Mix the cornflour and sugar to a paste with the water. Pour the mixture into the pan. Cook, stirring, until the sauce has thickened. Season to taste with salt. Serve at once, with rice noodles.

ingredients

350g/12oz rump **steak**, trimmed
and thinly sliced

15ml/1 tbsp **vegetable oil**

300ml/½ pint/1¼ cups
beef stock

2 **garlic** cloves, finely chopped

5ml/1 tsp grated fresh
root ginger

1 fresh **red chilli**, seeded
and finely chopped

15ml/1 tbsp **black bean sauce**

1 **green pepper**, seeded and cut
into 2.5cm/1in squares

15ml/1 tbsp **dry sherry**

5ml/1 tsp **cornflour**

5ml/1 tsp **caster sugar**

45ml/3 tbsp **water**

salt

rice noodles, to serve

cook's tip
For extra colour, use half each of a green pepper and red pepper or a mixture that includes yellow and orange peppers.

ingredients

350g/12oz rump
   steak, trimmed
15ml/1 tbsp **vegetable oil**
300ml/½ pint /1¼ cups
   beef stock
1 **garlic** clove, finely chopped
1 small **onion**, sliced into rings
5 **tomatoes**, quartered
15ml/1 tbsp **tomato purée**
5ml/1 tsp **caster sugar**
15ml/1 tbsp **dry sherry**
15ml/1 tbsp **water**
salt and freshly ground
   white pepper
noodles, to serve

beef with tomatoes

COLOURFUL AND **FRESH**-TASTING, THIS
IS THE PERFECT WAY OF SERVING **SUN-
RIPENED** TOMATOES FROM THE GARDEN.

method   SERVES 4

1 Slice the beef thinly. Place the slices in a bowl, add 5ml/1 tsp of the
vegetable oil and stir to coat.

2 Bring the stock to the boil in a saucepan. Add the beef and cook for
2 minutes, stirring constantly. Drain the beef and set it aside.

3 Heat the remaining oil in a frying pan or wok until very hot. Stir-fry the
garlic and onion for a few seconds.

4 Add the beef and tomatoes and cook for 1 minute more. Mix the
tomato purée, sugar, sherry and water in a cup or small bowl. Stir the
mixture into the pan, add salt and pepper to taste and mix thoroughly.
Cook for 1 minute, then serve with noodles.

vegetables

stir-fried beansprouts

THIS **FRESH**, **CRUNCHY** VEGETABLE, WHICH IS ALMOST SYNONYMOUS WITH CHINESE RESTAURANTS, TASTES SO **MUCH BETTER** WHEN **STIR-FRIED** AT HOME.

method

SERVES 4

1 Heat the vegetable oil in a frying pan or wok. Add the chopped garlic and grated ginger and stir-fry for a few minutes.

2 Add the bamboo shoot and carrot matchsticks to the pan or wok and stir-fry for a few minutes.

3 Add the beansprouts to the pan or wok with the salt and a pinch of pepper. Drizzle over the sherry and toss the beansprouts over the heat for 3 minutes until hot.

4 Sprinkle over the soy sauce and sesame oil, toss to mix thoroughly, then serve at once.

<table>
<tr><td>cook's tip</td></tr>
<tr><td>Beansprouts keep best when stored in the fridge or other cool place in a bowl of cold water, but you must remember to change the water daily.</td></tr>
</table>

ingredients

15ml/1 tbsp **vegetable oil**

1 **garlic** clove,
   finely chopped

5ml/1 tsp grated fresh
   root ginger

50g/2oz/½ cup drained, canned
   bamboo shoots, cut into
   fine matchsticks

1 small **carrot**, cut into
   fine matchsticks

450g/1lb/8 cups **beansprouts**

2.5ml/½ tsp **salt**

freshly ground **white pepper**

15ml/1 tbsp **dry sherry**

15ml/1 tbsp light **soy sauce**

2.5ml/½ tsp **sesame oil**

ingredients

450g/1lb **green beans**

15ml/1 tbsp **vegetable oil**

3 **garlic** cloves, finely chopped

5 **spring onions**, cut into
    2.5cm/1in lengths

25g/1oz **dried shrimp**, soaked
    in warm water and drained

15ml/1 tbsp light **soy sauce**

salt

sautéed green beans

THE **SMOKY** FLAVOUR OF THE DRIED SHRIMP ADDS AN **EXTRA DIMENSION** TO **GREEN BEANS** COOKED THIS WAY.

method

SERVES 4

1 Trim the green beans. Cut each green bean in half.

2 Bring a saucepan of lightly salted water to the boil and cook the beans for 3–4 minutes, until crisp-tender. Drain, refresh under cold water and drain again.

3 Heat the oil in a frying pan or wok until very hot. Stir-fry the garlic and spring onions for 30 seconds then add the shrimp. Mix lightly.

4 Add the green beans and soy sauce. Toss the mixture over the heat until the beans are hot. Serve at once.

cook's tip
Don't be tempted to use too many dried shrimp. Their flavour is very strong and could overwhelm the more delicate taste of the beans.

braised aubergine & courgettes

AUBERGINE, COURGETTES AND SOME FRESH **RED CHILLIES** FORM THE BASIS OF A VEGETARIAN DISH THAT IS **SIMPLE**, SPICY AND **QUITE SENSATIONAL**.

ingredients

method

SERVES 4

1 **aubergine**, about 350g/12oz

2 small **courgettes**

15ml/1 tbsp **vegetable oil**

2 **garlic** cloves, finely chopped

2 fresh **red chillies**, seeded and finely chopped

1 small **onion**, diced

15ml/1 tbsp **black bean sauce**

15ml/1 tbsp dark **soy sauce**

45ml/3 tbsp **cold water**

salt

chilli flowers (optional), to garnish (see cook's tip)

1 Trim the aubergine and slice it in half lengthways, then across into 1cm/½in thick slices. Layer the slices in a colander, sprinkling each layer with salt. Leave the aubergine in the sink to stand for about 20 minutes.

2 Roll-cut the courgettes by slicing off one end diagonally, then rolling the courgette through 180 degrees and taking off another diagonal slice, which will form a triangular wedge. Make more wedges of courgette in the same way.

3 Rinse the aubergine slices well, drain and dry thoroughly on absorbent kitchen paper.

4 Heat the oil in a wok or frying pan. Stir-fry the garlic, chillies and onion with the black bean sauce for a few seconds.

5 Add the aubergine slices and stir-fry for 2 minutes, sprinkling over a little water to prevent them from burning.

6 Stir in the courgettes, soy sauce and measured water. Cook, stirring occasionally, for 5 minutes. Serve hot, garnished with chilli flowers.

cook's tip

Chilli flowers make a pretty garnish. Using a small pair of scissors, slit a fresh red chilli from the tip to within 1cm/½in of the stem end. Repeat this at regular intervals around the chilli so that you have slender "petals" attached at the stem. Rinse the chilli to remove the seeds, then place it in a bowl of iced water for at least 4 hours, until the "petals" curl.

broccoli with soy sauce

A **WONDERFULLY** SIMPLE DISH THAT YOU WILL WANT TO MAKE **AGAIN** AND **AGAIN**. THE BROCCOLI COOKS IN MINUTES, SO DON'T START COOKING UNTIL YOU ARE ALMOST **READY** TO EAT.

ingredients

450g/1lb **broccoli**
15ml/1 tbsp **vegetable oil**
2 **garlic** cloves, crushed
30ml/2 tbsp light **soy sauce**
salt
fried **garlic** slices, to garnish

variation

Most leafy vegetables taste delicious prepared this way. Try blanched Cos lettuce and you may be surprised at how crisp and clean the taste is.

method

SERVES 4

1 Trim and discard the thick stems of the broccoli and then cut the head part into large florets.

2 Bring a saucepan of lightly salted water to the boil. Add the broccoli and cook for 3–4 minutes until crisp-tender. Drain thoroughly and arrange in a heated serving dish.

3 Heat the oil in a small saucepan. Fry the garlic for 2 minutes to release the flavour, then remove it with a slotted spoon. Pour the oil carefully over the broccoli, taking care as it will splatter. Drizzle the soy sauce over the broccoli, scatter over the fried garlic slices and serve.

ingredients

675g/1½lb **Chinese leaves**

15ml/1 tbsp **vegetable oil**

2 **garlic** cloves, finely chopped

2.5cm/1in piece of fresh **root ginger**, finely chopped

2.5ml/½ tsp **salt**

15ml/1 tbsp **oyster sauce**

4 **spring onions**, cut into 2.5cm/1in lengths

stir-fried chinese leaves

THIS SIMPLE WAY OF COOKING **CHINESE LEAVES** PRESERVES THEIR **DELICATE FLAVOUR**.

method

SERVES 4

1 Stack the Chinese leaves together and cut them into 2.5cm/1in slices.

2 Heat the oil in a wok or large deep saucepan. Stir-fry the garlic and ginger for 1 minute.

3 Add the Chinese leaves to the wok or saucepan and stir-fry for 2 minutes. Sprinkle the salt over and drizzle with the oyster sauce. Toss the leaves over the heat for 2 minutes more.

4 Stir in the spring onions. Toss the mixture well, transfer it to a heated serving plate and serve.

> cook's tip
> For guests who are vegetarian, substitute 15ml/1 tbsp light soy sauce and 5ml/1 tsp caster sugar for the oyster sauce.

mixed vegetables monk-style

CHINESE MONKS EAT NEITHER **MEAT** NOR **FISH**, SO "MONK-STYLE" DISHES ARE IDEAL FOR **VEGETARIANS**.

ingredients

50g/2oz dried **tofu**
   (beancurd) sticks
115g/4oz fresh **lotus root**, or
   50g/2oz dried
10g/1/4oz dried **wood ears**
8 dried **Chinese mushrooms**
15ml/1 tbsp **vegetable oil**
75g/3oz/3/4 cup drained, canned
   straw mushrooms
115g/4oz/1 cup **baby corn
   cobs**, cut in half
30ml/2 tbsp light **soy sauce**
15ml/1 tbsp **dry sherry**
10ml/2 tsp **caster sugar**
150ml/1/4 pint/2/3 cup
   vegetable stock
75g/3oz **mangetouts**, trimmed
   and cut in half
5ml/1 tsp **cornflour**
15ml/ 1tbsp **water**
salt

cook's tip
The flavour of this tasty mix improves on keeping, so any leftovers would taste even better next day.

method

SERVES 4

1 Put the tofu (beancurd) sticks in a bowl. Cover with hot water and leave to soak for 1 hour. If using fresh lotus root, peel and slice it; if using dried lotus root, place in a bowl of hot water and leave to soak for 1 hour.

2 Prepare the wood ears and dried Chinese mushrooms by soaking them in separate bowls of hot water for 15 minutes. Drain the wood ears, trim off and discard the hard base from each and cut the rest into bite-size pieces. Drain the soaked mushrooms, trim off and discard the stems and chop the caps roughly.

3 Drain the tofu (beancurd) sticks. Cut them into 5cm/2in long pieces, discarding any hard pieces. If using dried lotus root, drain well.

4 Heat the oil in a frying pan or wok. Stir-fry the wood ears, Chinese mushrooms and lotus root for about 30 seconds.

5 Add the pieces of tofu (beancurd), straw mushrooms, baby corn cobs, soy sauce, sherry, caster sugar and stock. Bring to the boil, then cover the pan or wok, lower the heat and simmer for about 20 minutes.

6 Stir in the mangetouts with salt to taste, and cook, uncovered, for 2 minutes more. Mix the cornflour to a paste with the water. Add the mixture to the pan or wok. Cook, stirring, until the sauce thickens. Serve at once.

braised tofu with mushrooms

THE **MARINADE** AND **MUSHROOMS** FLAVOUR THE TOFU
BEAUTIFULLY IN THIS **PERFECT** VEGETARIAN MAIN COURSE.

ingredients

350g/12oz **tofu** (beancurd)
2.5ml/1/2 tsp **sesame oil**
10ml/2 tsp light **soy sauce**
15ml/1 tbsp **vegetable oil**
2 **garlic** cloves, finely chopped
2.5ml/1/2 tsp grated fresh
   root ginger
115g/4oz/1 cup fresh
   shiitake mushrooms,
   stalks removed
175g/6oz/11/2 cups **fresh**
   oyster mushrooms
115g/4oz/1 cup drained, canned
   straw mushrooms
115g/4oz/1 cup **button**
   mushrooms, cut in half
15ml/1 tbsp **dry sherry**
15ml/1 tbsp dark **soy sauce**
90ml/6 tbsp **vegetable stock**
5ml/1 tsp **cornflour**
15ml/1 tbsp **water**
salt and freshly ground
   white pepper
2 **spring onions**, shredded,
   to garnish

method

SERVES 4

1 Put the tofu in a dish and sprinkle with the sesame oil, light soy sauce and a large pinch of pepper. Leave to marinate for 10 minutes, then drain and cut into 2.5 x 1cm/1 x 1/2in pieces.

2 Heat the vegetable oil in a frying pan or wok. When it is very hot, fry the garlic and ginger for a few seconds. Add all the mushrooms and stir-fry for 2 minutes.

3 Stir in the sherry, soy sauce and stock, with salt, if needed, and pepper. Simmer for 4 minutes.

4 Mix the cornflour to a paste with the water. Stir the mixture into the pan or wok and cook, stirring, until thickened.

5 Carefully add the pieces of tofu, toss gently to coat thoroughly and simmer for 2 minutes.

6 Scatter the shredded spring onions over the top of the mixture, transfer to a serving dish and serve immediately.

cook's tip
If fresh shiitake mushrooms are not available, use dried Chinese mushrooms soaked in hot water. Use the soaking liquid instead of vegetable stock for a more intense flavour.

rice & noodles

festive rice

THIS **ATTRACTIVE** RICE DISH IS TRADITIONALLY **SHAPED** INTO A CONE AND SURROUNDED BY A **VARIETY OF ACCOMPANIMENTS** BEFORE BEING SERVED.

method

SERVES 8

1 Put the rice in a strainer and rinse thoroughly under cold running water. Drain well.

2 Heat the oil in a frying pan that has a lid. Fry the garlic, onions and turmeric over a low heat for a few minutes, until the onions are softened, but not browned. Add the rice and stir well so that each grain is thoroughly coated.

3 Pour in the water and coconut milk and add the lemon grass. Bring to the boil, stirring well. Cover the pan and leave to cook gently for 15–20 minutes, or until all the liquid has been absorbed.

4 Remove the pan from the heat and lift the lid. Cover with a clean dish towel, replace the lid and leave to stand in a warm place for 15 minutes. Remove the lemon grass, mound the rice mixture into a cone on a serving platter and garnish with the accompaniments. Serve immediately.

> ### cook's tip
> Look for fresh turmeric at Asian markets or food stores. It is a rhizome and looks rather like fresh root ginger.

ingredients

450g/1lb/2⅓ cups
 fragrant rice
60ml/4 tbsp **oil**
2 **garlic** cloves, crushed
2 **onions**, finely sliced
5cm/2in piece of **fresh
 turmeric**, peeled and crushed
750ml/1¼ pints/3 cups **water**
400ml/14fl oz can **coconut milk**
1–2 lemon **grass stalks**,
 bruised

For the accompaniments
omelette strips
2 fresh **red chillies**, shredded
cucumber chunks
tomato wedges
deep-fried **onions**
prawn crackers

ingredients

225g/8oz/1⅓ cups **black glutinous rice** or **brown rice**

900ml/1½ pints/3¾ cups **vegetable stock**

15ml/1 tbsp **vegetable oil**

225g/8oz **Chinese leaves**, cut into 1cm/½in strips

4 **spring onions**, thinly sliced

salt and freshly ground **white pepper**

2.5ml/½ tsp sesame oil

chinese leaves & black rice stir-fry

THE **SLIGHTLY NUTTY**, CHEWY BLACK **GLUTINOUS RICE** CONTRASTS BEAUTIFULLY WITH THE CHINESE LEAVES.

method

SERVES 4

1 Rinse the rice until the water runs clear, then drain and tip into a saucepan. Add the stock and bring to the boil. Lower the heat, cover the pan and cook gently for 30 minutes. Remove from the heat and leave to stand for 15 minutes without lifting the pan lid.

2 Heat the vegetable oil in a frying pan or wok. Stir-fry the Chinese leaves for 2 minutes, sprinkling with a little water to prevent them from burning.

3 Drain the rice, stir it into the pan and cook for 4 minutes, using two spatulas or spoons to toss it with the Chinese leaves over the heat.

4 Add the spring onions, with salt and pepper to taste and the sesame oil. Cook for 1 minute more. Serve at once.

fried rice with mushrooms

A **TASTY RICE** DISH THAT IS ALMOST A MEAL IN ITSELF. **SESAME** OIL ADDS A **HINT** OF **NUTTY FLAVOUR**.

ingredients

225g/8oz/1¼ cups **long grain rice**
15ml/1 tbsp **vegetable oil**
1 **egg**, lightly beaten
2 **garlic** cloves, crushed
175g/6oz/1¼ cups **button mushrooms**, sliced
15ml/1 tbsp **light soy sauce**
1.5ml/¼ tsp **salt**
2.5ml/½ tsp **sesame oil**
cucumber matchsticks, to garnish

cook's tip

When you cook rice this way, you may find there is a crust at the bottom of the pan. Simply soak the crust in water for a couple of minutes to break it up, then drain it and fry it with the rest of the rice.

method

SERVES 4

1 Rinse the rice until the water runs clear, then drain. Place it in a saucepan. Measure the depth of the rice against your index finger, then bring the finger up to just above the surface of the rice and add cold water to the same depth as the rice.

2 Bring the water to the boil. Stir, boil for a few minutes, then cover the pan. Lower the heat to a simmer and cook the rice gently for 5–8 minutes, until all the water has been absorbed. Remove the pan from the heat and, without lifting the lid, leave for another 10 minutes before stirring or forking up the rice.

3 Heat 5ml/1 tsp of the vegetable oil in a frying pan or wok. Add the egg and cook, stirring with a chopstick or wooden spoon until scrambled. Remove and set aside.

4 Heat the remaining vegetable oil in the clean pan or wok. Stir-fry the garlic for a few seconds, then add the mushrooms and stir-fry for 2 minutes, adding a little water, if needed, to prevent burning.

5 Stir in the cooked rice and cook, stirring occasionally, for 4 minutes, or until the rice is hot.

6 Add the scrambled egg, soy sauce, salt and sesame oil. Cook for 1 minute to heat through. Serve immediately, garnished with cucumber matchsticks.

sticky rice parcels

THIS **SUPERB** DISH IS **PACKED** WITH **FLAVOUR**. THE PARCELS LOOK PRETTY AND ARE A **PLEASURE** TO **EAT**.

method

SERVES 4

1 Rinse the glutinous rice until the water runs clear, then leave to soak in water for 2 hours. Drain and stir in 5ml/1 tsp of the oil and 2.5ml/½ tsp salt. Line a large steamer with a piece of clean muslin. Transfer the rice into this. Cover and steam over boiling water for 45 minutes, stirring the rice from time to time and topping up the water if needed.

2 Mix the soy sauce, five-spice powder and sherry. Put the chicken pieces in a bowl, add the marinade, stir to coat, then cover and leave to marinate for 20 minutes.

3 Drain the Chinese mushrooms, cut out and discard the stems, then chop the caps roughly. Drain the dried shrimp. Heat the remaining oil in a frying pan or wok. Stir-fry the chicken for 2 minutes, then add the mushrooms, shrimp, bamboo shoots and stock. Lower the heat and allow to simmer for 10 minutes.

4 Mix the cornflour to a paste with the water. Add the mixture to the pan and cook, stirring, until the sauce has thickened. Season with salt and white pepper to taste. Lift the cooked rice out of the steamer and leave it to cool slightly.

5 With lightly dampened hands, divide the rice into four equal portions. Put half of one portion in the centre of a lotus leaf. Spread it into a round and place a quarter of the chicken mixture on top. Cover with the remaining half portion of rice. Fold the leaf around the filling to make a neat rectangular parcel. Make three more parcels in the same way.

6 Prepare a steamer. Put the rice parcels, seam side down, into the steamer. Cover and steam over a high heat for about 30 minutes. Serve the parcels on individual heated plates, inviting the diners to unwrap their own parcels.

ingredients

450g/1lb/2⅔ cups
  glutinous rice
20ml/4 tsp **vegetable oil**
15ml/1 tbsp dark **soy sauce**
1.5ml/¼ tsp Chinese **five-spice powder**
15ml/1 tbsp **dry sherry**
4 skinless boneless **chicken** thighs, each cut into 4 pieces
8 dried **Chinese mushrooms,** soaked in hot water until soft
25g/1oz **dried shrimp**, soaked in hot water until soft
50g/2oz/½ cup sliced, drained, canned **bamboo shoots**
300ml/½ pint/1¼ cups **chicken stock**
10ml/2 tsp **cornflour**
15ml/1 tbsp **cold water**
4 **lotus leaves**, soaked in warm water until soft
salt and freshly ground **white pepper**

ingredients

50g/2oz cooked **ham**

50g/2oz cooked **prawns**,
  peeled and deveined

3 **eggs**

5ml/1 tsp **salt**

2 **spring onions**, finely chopped

115g/4oz/1 cup **green peas**,
  thawed if frozen

60ml/4 tbsp **vegetable oil**

15ml/1 tbsp light **soy sauce**

15ml/1 tbsp **Chinese rice wine**
  or **dry sherry**

450g/1lb/4 cups cooked **rice**

chinese fried rice

CHINESE **FRIED RICE** IS MORE **ELABORATE**
THAN THE MORE FAMILIAR EGG FRIED RICE,
AND IS ALMOST A **MEAL** IN **ITSELF**.

method

SERVES 4

1 Dice the ham finely. Pat the prawns dry on kitchen paper.

2 In a bowl, beat the eggs lightly with a pinch of the salt and a few
  pieces of the spring onions.

3 Heat about half the oil in a wok or frying pan, stir-fry the peas, prawns
and ham for 1 minute, then add the soy sauce and wine or sherry.
Transfer to a bowl and keep hot.

4 Heat the remaining oil in the wok or pan and scramble the eggs
lightly. Add the rice and stir to make sure that each grain of rice is
separate. Add the remaining salt, the remaining spring onions and the
prawn mixture. Toss over the heat to mix. Serve hot or cold.

variations
This is one of those good-tempered recipes that are ideal for using up
leftovers. Use cooked chicken or turkey instead of the ham, doubling the
quantity if you omit the prawns.

special fried rice

THIS DELICIOUS RECIPE COMBINES **CHICKEN**, **SHRIMP** AND **VEGETABLES** WITH FRIED RICE. LETTUCE AND A **SPRINKLING** OF NUTS ARE ADDED FOR **EXTRA CRUNCH**.

ingredients

175g/6oz/scant 1 cup **long grain white rice**
45ml/3 tbsp **groundnut oil**
350ml/12fl oz/1½ cups **water**
1 **garlic** clove, crushed
4 **spring onions**, finely chopped
115g/4oz/1 cup diced cooked **chicken**
115g/4oz/1 cup cooked peeled **shrimp**, rinsed if canned
1 **egg**, beaten with a pinch of **salt**
50g/2oz/1 cup shredded **lettuce**
30ml/2 tbsp light **soy sauce**
pinch of **caster sugar**
salt and freshly ground **black pepper**
roasted **cashew nuts** and **fresh herbs**, to garnish

method

SERVES 4

1 Rinse the rice in two to three changes of warm water to wash away some of the starch. Drain well.

2 Put the rice in a saucepan and add 15ml/1 tbsp of the oil. Pour in the measured water. Bring to the boil, stir once, then cover and simmer for 12–15 minutes, until nearly all the water has been absorbed. Switch off the heat and leave, covered, to stand for 10 minutes. Fluff up with a fork and leave to cool.

3 Heat the remaining oil in a frying pan or wok, add the garlic and spring onions and stir-fry for 30 seconds.

4 Add the chicken and shrimp and stir-fry for 1–2 minutes, then add the cooked rice and stir-fry for 2 minutes more. Pour in the egg and stir-fry until just set. Stir in the lettuce, soy sauce and sugar and season to taste with salt and pepper.

5 Transfer to a warm serving bowl, garnish with the cashew nuts and herbs and serve immediately, with more soy sauce, if liked.

chinese jewelled rice

ANOTHER **FRIED RICE MEDLEY**, THIS TIME WITH CRAB MEAT
AND WATER CHESTNUTS PROVIDING **CONTRASTING TEXTURES**
AND **FLAVOURS**.

ingredients

350g/12oz/1¾ cups **long
 grain rice**
45ml/3 tbsp **vegetable oil**
1 **onion**, roughly chopped
4 dried **black Chinese
 mushrooms**, soaked for
 10 minutes in warm water
115g/4oz cooked **ham**, diced
175g/6oz drained canned **white
 crab meat**
75g/3oz/½ cup drained canned
 water chestnuts, cubed
115g/4oz/1 cup **peas**, thawed
 if frozen
30ml/2 tbsp **oyster sauce**
5ml/1 tsp **sugar**
salt

method

SERVES 4

1 Rinse the rice, then cook for 10–12 minutes in a saucepan of lightly
 salted boiling water. Drain, refresh under cold water and drain again.
 Heat half the oil in a wok or frying pan. When very hot, stir-fry the
 rice for 3 minutes. Transfer to a bowl and set aside.

2 Heat the remaining oil in the wok and cook the onion until softened
 but not coloured. Drain the mushrooms, cut off and discard the stems,
 then chop the caps.

3 Add the chopped mushrooms to the wok, with all the remaining
 ingredients except the rice. St r-fry for 2 minutes, then add the rice
 and stir-fry for 3 minutes more. Serve at once.

---

cook's tip
When adding the oil to the hot wck, drizzle it in a "necklace" just below the
rim. As it runs down, it will coat the inner surface as it heats.

toasted noodles with vegetables

CRISP NOODLE **CAKES** TOPPED WITH VEGETABLES MAKE AN **UNUSUAL** AND **TASTY** SUPPER DISH.

method

SERVES 4

1 Bring a saucepan of water to the boil. Add the egg vermicelli and cook according to the instructions on the packet until just tender. Drain, refresh under cold water, drain again, then dry thoroughly on absorbent kitchen paper.

2 Heat 2.5ml/1/2 tsp of the oil in a frying pan or wok. When it starts to smoke, spread half the noodles over the base. Fry for 2–3 minutes, until lightly toasted. Turn the noodles over (they stick together like a cake), fry the other side, then slide on to a heated serving plate. Repeat with the remaining noodles to make 2 cakes. Keep hot.

3 Heat the remaining oil in the clean pan or wok, then fry the garlic for a few seconds. Halve the corn cobs lengthways, add to the pan with the mushrooms, then stir-fry for 3 minutes, adding water to prevent burning. Add the celery, carrot, mangetouts and bamboo shoots. Stir-fry for 2 minutes, until the vegetables are tender-crisp.

4 Mix the cornflour to a paste with the water. Add the mixture to the pan or wok with the soy sauce, sugar and vegetable stock. Cook, stirring, until the sauce thickens. Season to taste with salt and white pepper. Divide the vegetable mixture between the noodle cakes, garnish with the spring onion curls and serve. Each noodle cake serves 2 people.

ingredients

175g/6oz/1 1/2 cups dried
  egg vermicelli
15ml/1 tbsp **vegetable oil**
2 **garlic** cloves, finely chopped
115g/4 oz/1 cup **baby**
  corn cobs
115g/4oz/1 cup fresh **shiitake**
  mushrooms, halved
3 **celery** sticks, sliced
1 **carrot**, sliced diagonally
115g/4oz/1 cup **mangetouts**
75g/3oz/3/4 cup sliced, drained,
  canned **bamboo shoots**
15ml/1 tbsp **cornflour**
15ml/1 tbsp **water**
15ml/1 tbsp dark **soy sauce**
5ml/1 tsp **caster sugar**
300ml/1/2 pint/1 1/4 cups
  vegetable stock
salt and freshly ground
  white pepper
spring onion curls, to garnish

ingredients

175g/6oz/1½ cups **dried
 egg noodles**
15ml/1 tbsp **vegetable oil**
1 **garlic** clove, finely chopped
1 small **onion**, halved and sliced
225g/8oz/4 cups **beansprouts**
1 small **red pepper**, seeded and
 cut into strips
1 small **green pepper**, seeded
 and cut into strips
2.5ml/½ tsp **salt**
1.5ml/¼ tsp freshly ground
 white pepper
30ml/2 tbsp light **soy sauce**

stir-fried noodles with beansprouts

A **CLASSIC** CHINESE **NOODLE** DISH THAT IS
A MARVELLOUS **SIDE DISH**.

method

SERVES 4

1 Bring a saucepan of water to the boil. Cook the noodles for
 4 minutes, until just tender, or according to the instructions on the
 packet. Drain, refresh under cold water and drain again.

2 Heat the oil in a frying pan or wok. When the oil is very hot, add the
 garlic, stir briefly, then add the onion slices. Cook, stirring constantly,
 for 1 minute, then add the beansprouts and peppers. Stir-fry for
 2–3 minutes.

3 Stir in the cooked noodles and toss over the heat, using two spatulas
 or wooden spoons, for 2–3 minutes, or until the ingredients are well
 mixed and have heated through.

4 Add the salt, pepper and soy sauce and stir thoroughly before serving
 the noodle mixture in heated bowls.

ingredients

2 **duck** breasts

15ml/1 tbsp **vegetable oil**

150g/5oz **sugar snap peas**

2 **carrots**, cut into 7.5cm/
3in sticks

225g/8oz medium **egg noodles**

6 **spring onions**, sliced

salt

30ml/2 tbsp **coriander leaves**,
to garnish

For the marinade

15ml/1 tbsp **sesame oil**

5ml/1 tsp ground **coriander**

5ml/1 tsp Chinese **five-
spice powder**

For the dressing

15ml/1 tbsp **garlic vinegar**

5ml/1 tsp light **brown sugar**

5ml/1 tsp light **soy sauce**

15ml/1 tbsp toasted **sesame
seeds** (see cook's tip)

45ml/3 tbsp **sunflower oil**

30ml/2 tbsp **sesame oil**

freshly ground **black pepper**

sesame duck &
noodle salad

THIS SALAD IS A COMPLETE MEAL IN ITSELF
AND MAKES A LOVELY **SUMMER LUNCH**.
THE **MARINADE** IS A SUPERB BLEND OF
DELICIOUS **SPICES.**

method
SERVES 4

1 Slice the duck breasts thinly across the grain and place them in a
shallow dish. Mix together all the ingredients for the marinade, pour
over the duck and mix well to coat thoroughly. Cover and leave in a
cool place for 30 minutes.

2 Heat the oil in a frying pan or wok, add the slices of duck breast and
stir-fry for 3–4 minutes, until cooked. Set aside.

3 Bring a saucepan of lightly salted water to the boil. Place the sugar
snap peas and carrots in a steamer that will fit on top of the pan.
When the water boils, add the noodles. Place the steamer on top
and steam the vegetables, while cooking the noodles for the time
suggested on the packet. Set the steamed vegetables aside. Drain
the noodles, refresh them under cold running water and drain again.
Place them in a large serving bowl.

4 Make the dressing. Mix the vinegar, sugar, soy sauce and sesame
seeds in a bowl. Add a generous grinding of black pepper, then whisk
in the oils.

5 Pour the dressing over the noodles and mix well. Add the sugar snap
peas, carrots, spring onions and duck slices and toss to mix. Scatter
the coriander leaves over and serve.

---

cook's tip

To toast the sesame seeds, place them in a dry heavy-based pan and heat
gently, stirring frequently, until they are lightly browned.

---

singapore rice vermicelli

SIMPLE AND **SPEEDILY** PREPARED, THIS LIGHTLY **CURRIED** RICE NOODLE DISH IS A **FULL MEAL** IN A BOWL.

ingredients

225g/8oz/2 cups dried
  rice vermicelli
15ml/1 tbsp **vegetable oil**
1 **egg**, lightly beaten
2 **garlic** cloves, finely chopped
1 large fresh **red** or **green**
  chilli, seeded and
  finely chopped
15ml/1 tbsp medium
  curry powder
1 **red pepper**, seeded and
  thinly sliced
1 **green pepper**, seeded and
  thinly sliced
1 **carrot**, cut into matchsticks
1.5ml/1/2 tsp **salt**
60ml/4 tbsp **vegetable stock**
115g/4oz cooked peeled
  prawns, thawed if frozen
75g/3oz lean **ham**, cut into
  1cm/1/2in cubes
15ml/1 tbsp light **soy sauce**

method

SERVES 4

1 Soak the rice vermicelli in a bowl of boiling water for 4 minutes, or according to the instructions on the packet, then drain thoroughly and set aside.

2 Heat 5ml/1 tsp of the oil in a frying pan or wok. Add the egg and scramble until set. Remove with a slotted spoon and set aside.

3 Heat the remaining oil in the clean pan. Stir-fry the garlic and chilli for a few seconds, then stir in the curry powder. Cook for 1 minute, stirring, then stir in the peppers, carrot sticks, salt and stock.

4 Bring to the boil. Add the prawns, ham, scrambled egg, rice vermicelli and soy sauce. Mix well. Cook, stirring, until all the liquid has been absorbed and the mixture is hot. Serve at once.

seafood soup noodles

AUDIBLE SOUNDS OF **ENJOYMENT** ARE A COMPLIMENT TO THE CHINESE COOK, SO **SLURPING** THIS **SOUP** IS NOT ONLY **PERMISSIBLE**, IT IS POSITIVELY **DESIRABLE**.

ingredients

175g/6oz raw **tiger prawns**, peeled and deveined
225g/8oz **monkfish fillet**, cut into chunks
225g/8oz **salmon fillet**, cut into chunks
5ml/1 tsp **vegetable oil**
15ml/1 tbsp dry **white wine**
225g/8oz/2 cups dried **egg vermicelli**
1.2 litres/2 pints/5 cups **fish stock**
1 **carrot**, thinly sliced
225g/8oz **asparagus**, cut into 5cm/2in lengths
30ml/2 tbsp dark **soy sauce**
5ml/1 tsp **sesame oil**
salt and freshly ground **black pepper**
2 **spring onions**, cut into thin rings, to garnish

> ### variation
> Try this simple recipe using rice vermicelli for a slightly different texture and taste.

method

SERVES 4

1 Mix the prawns and fish in a bowl. Add the vegetable oil and wine with 1.5ml/¼ tsp salt and a little pepper. Mix lightly, cover and marinate in a cool place for 15 minutes.

2 Bring a large saucepan of water to the boil and cook the noodles for 4 minutes, until just tender, or according to the instructions on the packet. Drain the noodles thoroughly and divide among four serving bowls. Keep hot.

3 Bring the fish stock to the boil in a separate pan. Add the prawns and monkfish, cook for 1 minute, then add the salmon and cook for 2 minutes more.

4 Using a slotted spoon, lift the fish and prawns out of the stock, add to the noodles in the bowls and keep hot.

5 Strain the stock through a sieve lined with muslin or cheesecloth into a clean pan. Bring to the boil and cook the carrot and asparagus for 2 minutes, then add the soy sauce and sesame oil, with salt to taste. Stir well.

6 Pour the stock and vegetables over the noodles and seafood, garnish with the spring onions and serve.

desserts

golden steamed sponge cake

CAKES ARE **NOT TRADITIONALLY** SERVED FOR DESSERT IN CHINA, BUT THIS **LIGHT SPONGE** IS VERY **POPULAR** WITH DIM SUM AT TEAHOUSES.

method

SERVES 8

1 Sift the flour, baking powder and bicarbonate of soda into a bowl. Line an 18cm/7in diameter bamboo steamer or cake tin with non-stick baking parchment.

ingredients

175g/6oz/1½ cups **plain flour**
5ml/1 tsp **baking powder**
1.5ml/¼ tsp **bicarbonate of soda**
3 large **eggs**
115g/4oz/⅔ cup light **brown sugar**
45ml/3 tbsp **walnut oil**
30ml/2 tbsp **golden syrup**
5ml/1 tsp **vanilla essence**

2 In a mixing bowl, whisk the eggs with the sugar until thick and frothy. Beat in the oil and syrup, then let the mixture stand for about 30 minutes.

3 Add the dry ingredients to the egg mixture with the vanilla essence, beating rapidly to form a thick batter.

4 Pour the batter into the lined steamer or tin. Cover and steam over boiling water for 30 minutes, or until the sponge springs back when it is gently pressed with a finger. Allow to cool for a few minutes before serving.

ingredients

75g/3oz/6 tbsp **caster sugar**

300ml/½ pint/1¼ cups **white dessert wine**

thinly pared rind and juice of 1 **lemon**

7.5cm/3in piece of fresh **root ginger**, bruised

5 **star anise**

10 **cloves**

600ml/1 pint/2½ cups **water**

6 slightly unripe **pears**

25g/1oz/3 tbsp drained, **stem ginger** in syrup, sliced

fromage frais, to serve

pears with ginger & star anise

STAR ANISE AND GINGER GIVE A **REFRESHING TWIST** TO THESE POACHED PEARS. SERVE THEM **CHILLED**.

method

SERVES 4

1 Place the caster sugar, dessert wine, lemon rind and juice, fresh root ginger, star anise, cloves and water into a saucepan just large enough to hold the pears snugly in an upright position. Bring to the boil.

2 Meanwhile, peel the pears, leaving the stems intact. Add them to the wine mixture, making sure that they are totally immersed in the liquid.

3 Return the wine mixture to the boil, lower the heat, cover and simmer for 15–20 minutes, or until the pears are tender. Lift out the pears with a slotted spoon and place them in a heatproof dish. Boil the wine syrup rapidly until it is reduced by about half, then pour over the pears. Allow them to cool, then chill.

4 Cut the pears into thick slices and arrange these on four serving plates. Remove the ginger and whole spices from the wine sauce, stir in the stem ginger and spoon the sauce over the pears. Serve with fromage frais.

heavenly jellies with fruit

DELICATE, **VANILLA-FLAVOURED** JELLY, SET WITH **RIBBONS** OF EGG WHITE WITHIN IT, MAKES A **DELIGHTFUL** DESSERT SERVED WITH FRESH **FRUIT**.

method

SERVES 6

1 Put the agar agar into a saucepan. Add the boiling water, return to the boil and then lower the heat. Simmer the mixture for 10–15 minutes, stirring occasionally, until the agar agar has dissolved completely.

2 Stir in the sugar. As soon as it has dissolved, strain the syrup through a fine sieve placed over a bowl. Return the mixture to the saucepan.

3 Immediately stir in the vanilla essence, then gently pour in the egg white in a steady stream; the heat will cook the egg. Stir once to distribute the threads of cooked egg white.

4 Pour the mixture into a shallow 28 x 18cm/11 x 7in baking tray and allow to cool. The jelly will set at room temperature, but will set faster and taste better if it is transferred to the fridge as soon as it has cooled completely.

5 Cut the strawberries in halves or quarters. If using fresh lychees, peel them and remove the stones. Divide the fruit among six small serving dishes or cups.

6 Turn the jelly out of the tray and cut it into diamond shapes to serve with the strawberries and lychees.

ingredients

10g/¼oz **agar agar**
900ml/1½ pints/3¾ cups boiling **water**
115g/4oz/½ cup **caster sugar**
5ml/1 tsp **vanilla essence**
1 **egg** white, lightly beaten
225g/8oz/1½ cups fresh **strawberries**
450g/1lb **fresh lychees** or 475g/19oz can **lychees**, well drained

variation
The jelly can be made with equal amounts of coconut milk and water and served with mangoes for a more tropical taste.

USUALLY **SERVED WARM**, THIS IS A LIGHT AND **REFRESHING** "SOUP", POPULAR WITH **CHILDREN** AND **ADULTS ALIKE**.

ingredients

115g/4oz/²⁄₃ cup **tapioca**

1.5 litres/2¹⁄₂ pints/6¹⁄₄ cups **water**

225g/8oz **taro**

150g/5oz/²⁄₃ cup **rock sugar**

300ml/¹⁄₂ pint/1¹⁄₄ cups **coconut milk**

tapioca & taro pudding

method

SERVES 4–6

1 Rinse the tapioca, drain well, then put into a bowl with fresh water to cover. Leave to soak for 30 minutes.

2 Drain the tapioca and put it in a saucepan with 900ml/1¹⁄₂ pints/ 3³⁄₄ cups water. Bring to the boil, lower the heat and simmer for about 6 minutes, or until the tapioca is transparent. Drain, refresh under cold water, and drain again.

3 Peel the taro and cut it into diamond-shaped slices, about 1cm/¹⁄₂in thick. Pour the remaining water into a saucepan and bring it to the boil. Add the taro and cook for 10–15 minutes or until it is just tender.

4 Using a slotted spoon, lift out half of the taro slices and set them aside. Continue to cook the remaining taro until it is very soft. Tip the taro and cooking liquid into a food processor and process until completely smooth.

5 Return the taro "soup" to the clean pan; stir in the sugar and simmer, stirring occasionally, until the sugar has dissolved.

6 Stir in the tapioca, reserved taro and coconut milk. Cook for a few minutes. Serve immediately in heated bowls. Alternatively, cool and chill before serving.

cook's tip

Taro is a starchy tuber that tastes rather like a floury potato. If it is difficult to obtain, use sweet potato instead.

toffee apples

ALL THE **FLAVOUR** AND **TEXTURE** OF THIS CLASSIC CHINESE
DESSERT WITHOUT THE **FUSS** AND FAT OF **DEEP FRYING**.

ingredients

25g/1oz/2 tbsp **butter**
75ml/5 tbsp **cold water**
40g/1½oz/6 tbsp **plain flour**
1 **egg**
1 **dessert apple**
5ml/1 tsp **vegetable oil**
175g/6oz/¾ cup
   caster sugar
5ml/1 tsp **sesame seeds**

cook's tip
A slightly unripe, firm banana can
be used instead of an apple to
ring the changes.

method

SERVES 6

1 Preheat the oven to 200°C/400°F/Gas 6. Put the butter and water
into a small saucepan and bring to the boil. Remove from the heat and
add the flour all at once. Stir vigorously until the mixture forms a
smooth paste which leaves the sides of the pan clean.

2 Cool the choux paste for 5 minutes, then beat in the egg, mixing
thoroughly until the mixture is smooth and glossy.

3 Peel and core the apple and cut it into 1cm/½in chunks.

4 Stir the apple into the choux paste and place teaspoonfuls on a
dampened non-stick baking sheet. Bake for 20–25 minutes, until
brown and crisp on the outside, but still soft inside.

5 When the pastries are cooked, heat the oil in a saucepan over a low
heat and add the caster sugar. Cook, without stirring, until the sugar
has melted and turned golden brown, then sprinkle in the sesame
seeds. Remove the pan from the heat.

6 Have ready a bowl of iced water. Add the pastries, a few at a time, to
the caramel and toss to coat them all over. Remove with a slotted
spoon and quickly dip in the iced water to set the caramel; drain well.
Serve immediately. If the caramel becomes too thick before all the
choux pastries have been coated, re-heat it gently until it liquefies
before continuing coating the pastries.

index